THE TEACHER'S BOOK OF AFFECTIVE INSTRUCTION

A Competency Based Approach

Richard B. Smith
Northern Illinois University

UNIVERSITY
PRESS OF
AMERICA

LANHAM • NEW YORK • LONDON

Copyright © 1987 by

University Press of America,® Inc.

4720 Boston Way
Lanham, MD 20706

3 Henrietta Street
London WC2E 8LU England

Printed in the United States of America

British Cataloging in Publication Information Available

Library of Congress Cataloging-in-Publication Data

Smith, Richard B., 1931-
   The teacher's book of affective instruction.

   Instructor's manual available.
   Includes bibliographies and index.
   1. Teaching.   2. Competency based education.
3. Operant conditioning.   4. Reinforcement
(Psychology)   5. Learning, Psychology of.
I. Title.
LB1027.S622   1987   371.1'02   87-14223
ISBN 0-8191-6483-6 (pbk. : alk. paper)

All University Press of America books are produced on acid-free
paper which exceeds the minimum standards set by the National
Historical Publication and Records Commission.

TABLE OF CONTENTS

Preface

The Teacher's Book of Affective Instruction has been developed as a direct result of an on-going competency-based approach to affective instruction. The text was written for the purpose of providing a means through which affective goals can be attained.

Educators are aware of the importance of attaining affective goals. About half the goals on any list of educational goals are affective. We readily recognize that if we are not successful in attaining our affective goals, we are going to be only minimally successful in attaining our cognitive and psychomotor goals.

However, in spite of the importance attributed to them, affective goals are not having much impact on educational practice. The goals which are present during initial instructional planning erode. After being listed on the statements of goals and purposes of our schools, no learning experiences typically are provided to lead to their attainment. The goals erode primarily because it is not clear how they can be attained. We are unsure of what needs to be done to give our students positive self-concepts, independence, or an appreciation of art, music, literature, mathematics, or science.

The text provides a practical model that can be used to help make affective goals attainable. The purpose is to help move affective instruction from the realm of incidental instruction to the realm of planned instruction. In the text an attempt is made to introduce and answer the problems and objections that are encountered along the way to developing sound affective instruction.

Use of the Text as a Supplemental Text

The text is constructed so that it can be used as a supplemental text in any course that deals with affective instruction, affective learning, or affective objectives. It can be used either as a text to introduce and facilitate discussions of affective instruction or it can be used in conjunction with exercises and test items in the "Teacher's Guide" to develop a competency based approach to affective instruction. The competency based approach changes the task of the instructor from one of presenting information to one of interacting with students about specific affective instructional problems. This approach is designed to get the students to the point where they can establish affective goals, reduce them to affective objectives, design learning experiences and evaluate the affective outcomes.

In using the text as a competency-based approach to the attainment of affective objectives, it is suggested that the following five-step approach be taken to each of the chapters:

Step 1: Discovering the problem. Each chapter begins with a "Discovering the Problem" episode. The purpose of the episode is to involve the students in a discussion of the major problem to be dealt with in the chapter. The problem acts as an "advanced organizer" to establish the problem in the mind of the student. When the students are placed in small groups, they can usually discover the problem in a few minutes. It is helpful if the students are able to formulate their own statement of the problem.

Step 2: Examining the objectives and reading the chapter. Specific behavioral objectives have been placed at the beginning of each chapter. The objectives point out what the students should be able to do after they have read the chapter. The objectives should be studied before reading the chapter to determine what is to be learned, and after reading the chapter, to determine if the objectives have been accomplished.

Step 3: The test. After the chapter has been read, the students can take a test over the objectives for the chapter. The "Teacher's Guide" to the text contains three test items that can be used to evaluate the attainment of each objective. The view that the author has taken is that the test is merely an extension of the learning experience. For this reason, the tests have been administered as "open book" tests, and the students given ample time to complete them. At this point, the tests are not used as a basis for assigning grades. Later, after the completion of the text, the items related to the attainment of important objectives are incorporated into a test for grading purposes.

Step 4: Scoring and correcting the test. The test which consists of three test items for each objective is scored by using a "punched out" overlay. By arranging the three test items for each objective so that the answers fall either directly above or directly across from each other, the instructor can quickly score the tests by objective. Different approaches have been used for scoring the attainment of the objectives. Some instructors have required three correct responses out of three before credit is given for the attainment of the objectives. Others have given credit for the objectives if the student gets two out of the three test items for an objective correct.

The tests are scored by having the students write down the number of items correct for each objective. The students are then required to attempt to reanswer the items related to the missed objectives. If the objective is missed on the second trial, the instructor discusses the missed items with the student.

Step 5: The worksheets, case studies, and discussions. The purpose of the worksheets, case studies, and discussions is to help the students see how the concepts and relationships that have been presented in the text can be applied in the classroom situation. The worksheets and case studies typically are done in small groups, and then discussed by the entire class.

Using the Text for the Inservice Training of Teachers

The use of the text for the inservice training of teachers generally requires a different approach from that used in the typical classroom. The inservice approach suggested below is constructed around six workshops that involve the teachers in role playing, discovery episodes, and practice exercises. An attempt has been made to minimize the amount of time that those conducting the workshops have to spend disseminating information and to maximize the amount of time the teachers are engaged in hands-on activities. It is not necessary, although it is helpful, if those attending the inservice sessions have read the related chapters. Those conducting the sessions, however, should have read both the related chapters and the discussions of the exercises contained in the "Teacher's Guide" so that they can anticipate the questions that are likely to arise. The series of workshops are listed below.

Discovering the Problem I: Parts 1 and 2 (Page 2)

Activity: Role-Playing Exercise

Time: Approximately 2 hours

Part 1--Purpose:

The purpose of part 1 is to involve teachers in an activity that forces them to look at the big picture regarding what the schools should be doing for students. The active participation in the role playing episode is designed to put teachers in touch with their philosophical beliefs regarding the nature of men and women, the needs of society, and the relationship of the schools to society. The exercise is designed to require the teachers to take a philosophical position, a process that causes their philosophy to become a working tool rather than a philosophical ornament.

Part 2--Purpose:

The purpose of part 2 is to involve the teachers in the process of making a comparison between the school goals they have derived, and those in Appendix A or the goals of their own school system. The teachers are usually surprised to find how closely the different sets of goals approximate each other.

The process of getting the teachers to rank the 10 goals that they feel are most important is useful because it helps them to discover the high value they assign to affective objectives. In addition, they discover the problem--the highly valued affective objectives are being allowed to erode because few learning experiences are presented to lead to their attainment. This, in turn, raises the question, "Why?"

Inservice Workshop II

Practice Exercise 1-3 (Page 25)

Purpose:

The purpose of the activity is to get the teachers involved in the process of 1) determining the affective goals that relate closely to their area of interest, 2) reducing their affective goals to behaviors, and 3) constructing specific affective objectives so that they are attainable.

Activity: The activity involves small group work involving teachers from the same or similar areas in the process of stating and systematically reducing affective goals to specific affective objectives.

Time: Approximately 2 to 3 hours. It will take longer if the goal is to be a final list of specific affective objectives.

Practice Exercise 2-2 (Page 45)

Purpose:

The purpose of the activities is to make teachers aware of the types of signal learning episodes that are currently occurring incidentally in the everyday functioning of the school. The completion of the exercise should help to explain how we are turning ourselves, our subject matter, and other school related activities into conditioned aversive stimuli.

Activities:

1. The first activity consists of a brief presentation and diagramming of Watson's conditioning and reconditioning experiment with Albert and the white rabbit. In the presentation, point out the conditions necessary for signal learning to occur, the nature of the response, the part played by the motivation of the learner, and the nature of reconditioning. This should not take longer than 20 minutes.

2. The second activity consists of small group work in which the teachers attempt 1) to diagram and label the signal learning experiences that the students have been exposed to in Practice Exercise 2-2, and 2) to diagram or write a short paragraph to explain what needs to be done to recondition the undesirable signal learning that has already occurred.

Time: Approximately 2 hours.

<u>Inservice</u> <u>Workshop</u> <u>IV</u>

Practice Exercise 3-4 (Page 76)

Purpose:

The purpose of the activity is to help teachers discover how they are providing learning experiences that ultimately cause their students to escape or withdraw from the desirable learning experiences provided in the schools.

Activities:

1. The first activity consists of a brief discussion of operant learning and the concepts of positive reinforcement, negative reinforcement, punishment, extinction, and escape and withdrawal behaviors. This should be followed by the diagramming and labeling of a sample diagram from question 1 to illustrate 1) how through signal learning school and school-related objects and activities become conditioned aversive stimuli, and 2) how negative reinforcement leads to the strengthening of behaviors that involve the escape or withdrawa from these activities.

2. The second activity consists of small group work in which the teachers attempt to diagram and label the signal learning episodes and subsequent escape behaviors contained in the exercise.

Time: Approximately 3 hours.

Practice Exercise 3-3 (Page 69)

Purpose:

The purpose of the case study is to give those involved practice in using concepts and relationships previously introduced in the process of analyzing and prescribing learning experiences for individual students. More specifically, the students are required to:

1. establish and justify their affective goals.

2. determine their positive and negative affective objectives.

3. determine the source of reinforcement for the undesired behaviors contained in their negative objectives.

4. discuss ways of extinguishing the undesired behaviors and strengthening the desired behaviors.

5. discuss the role of the peer group in bringing about the desired behaviors.

6. determine a way to make the desired behaviors self-reinforcing.

Activity: The Case Study of Carla.

Time: Three to four hours.

Practice Exercise 6 (Page 150)

Purpose:

   The purpose of Exercise 6 is to give those involved practice in establishing classroom conditions that will lead to the harnessing of peer reinforcement for the attainment of desired educational goals.

Activity: Establishing the Conditions for Harnessing Peer Reinforcement in the Classroom.

Time: Two to three hours.

CHAPTER 1

THE SCHOOLS AND AFFECTIVE INSTRUCTION

Behavioral Objectives for Chapter 1

When you have completed the chapter, you should be able to:

1. differentiate affective from cognitive and psychomotor goals.

2. identify statements that reflect the current status of affective goals in the schools.

3. given examples of different statements made by teachers, identify the teachers who have and have not fallen into the "Circular Trap of Underlying Causes."

4. identify new examples of hypothetical constructs.

5. given teacher statements, identify the teacher trying to change a hypothetical construct directly.

6. given teaching-learning situations, recognize when teachers are providing learning experiences that affect the attainment of their affective goals.

7. recognize the function of affective goals in the instructional process.

8. given statements regarding philosophical beliefs, recognize affective goals that are consistent with the beliefs.

9. differentiate between "growth" objectives and "classroom management" objectives.

10. given examples of different statements made by teachers, identify the most appropriate view of the negative behaviors that occur in the classroom.

11. given statements made by teachers, identify the teacher in the best position to bring about change in the student.

12. recognize the assumption involved in reducing affective goals to specific affective objectives.

13. identify the characteristics of specific affective objectives.

14. identify examples of appropriately stated specific affective objectives.

15. given an affective goal, identify the specific objective that contains behaviors that provide the best evidence of the attainment of the affective goal.

16. recognize the questions asked to a) derive a suggested list of behaviors, and b) determine whether or not the suggested objectives provide good evidence of the attainment of the affective goal.

17. recognize the characteristics of negative affective objectives.

18. given the teacher's affective objectives and examples of student behavior, identify the statement that best describes the teacher's task in determining learning experiences for the students.

19. identify "verbs" that are appropriate for use in specific affective objectives.

Discovering the Problem I

Part 1

Role-playing episode--Select five students from the class to act as school board members, and have the remainder of the class act as concerned parents. The task of this meeting of the school board and parents is to determine the goals of a new kindergarten through 12th grade school system. The school district in which this school functions is a microcosm of the United States. The chore of the parents in attempting to evolve the goals is to interact with the school board in such a way as to tell the board what they want the schools to do for their children. As these goals evolve, have them written on the board and discussed. A point that needs to be kept in mind is that at this point the emphasis is on the goals to be attained, and not on the means for attaining the goals.

Part 2

First, working individually, do the following:
In Appendix "A" there is a list of educational goals that have been suggested for American schools. Read the list of goals carefully. After you have read them, list the 10 goals that you think are most important for the schools to attain. What percentage of the goals that you selected were followed by an asterisk? For each goal followed by an asterisk, write a statement about why you think it was important. What characteristic do these goals have in common? What conclusion can you draw regarding the importance that the class as a whole assigned to these goals?

Second, working in groups or as a group, discuss the impact that these goals have had on the instructional process. To what degree are learning experiences provided specifically to the attainment to the goals? To what extent is their attainment evaluated? How do you explain this?

This book is written for teachers, prospective teachers, and administrators. It is concerned with how we can attain our important affective goals. The emphasis is on the attainment of affective goals which are concerned with the development of student interests, attitudes, appreciations, values, self-images, motivation, etc., rather than cognitive goals which are concerned with verbal and numerical learning or psychomotor goals which are concerned with the learning of motor skills.

We, as teachers, prospective teachers, and administrators are vitally concerned with the attainment of affective goals. The lists of educational goals that we construct nearly always contain statements indicating a desire to develop students who:

> are self-actualized.
> have positive self-concepts.
> appreciate the dignity and worth of others.
> are interested in new ideas.
> are self-directed learners.
> take pride in their work.
> cherish individual differences.
> are good citizens.

We naturally are interested in the attainment of these goals because we recognize that the continued growth of our students depends on our success in attaining them. Students who have poor self-concepts, an inability to relate to others, an aversion to reading, mathematics, literature, etc., are not likely to go on and achieve their potential.

In addition, we are interested in attaining affective goals not only because it is our job to promote the continued growth of our students, but because we genuinely like our students, and want them to grow into happy, productive citizens. We get the majority of our rewards from interacting with our students and watching them grow. The satisfaction that we feel when we see the withdrawn child begin to interact rewardingly with others; the mediocre student suddenly catch fire and begin to probe new ideas and solve new problems; the insecure student begin to make important decisions, or the creative student begin to take bold new steps, are very important to us.

The importance that we attach to the attainment of our affective goals is reflected in the lists of goals we generate whenever we are involved in attempting to determine the goals for our schools. Experience with these lists of educational goals generally indicates that any time we are involved in constructing these lists, about half of the goals that emerge are affective goals.

In addition to the goals mentioned above which are goals sought by all teachers, we as subject matter specialists also have a large number of affective goals we are trying to attain. The goals vary depending upon the subject matter being taught. Each subject matter area typically is viewed as making its own contribution to the affective development of the student. Listed below, next to the discipline, are examples of the affective goals that are often listed as desirable outcomes for the different disciplines.

Subject Matter Area	General Affective Objectives
1. Science	Develop students who: a. love nature b. appreciate the scientific method
2. English	Create students who: a. like literature

	b. have empathy for those of other races,

religions, and cultures

3. Mathematics   Develop students who:
                               a. enjoy solving number problems
                               b. appreciate the role of mathematics in their

lives

4. Social Studies   Create students who:
                               a. value democratic processes
                               b. appreciate the dignity and worth of people from

different backgrounds

5. Physical Education   Develop students who
                               a. like physical activity
                               b. value a healthy body

6. Art   Create students who:
                               a. enjoy creating their own works of art
                               b. appreciate the creative works of others

The sample lists given are far from complete. However, they illustrate the kinds of affective goals we are seeking to attain at both the school and classroom levels.

The Current Status of Our Affective Goals

In spite of the importance we attribute to the attainment of our affective goals, they have not had much impact on what we do in the classroom (Krathwohl, 1964). The objectives appear to function largely as ornaments that decorate our lists of goals—they look pretty, but have little effect on classroom practice. They are prevalent on every list of goals we construct. However, we typically design few learning experiences to lead to their attainment, and we seldom attempt to evaluate the effect that we are having on them.

We have two beliefs that are primary factors that lead to the erosion of our affective objectives (Bandura, 1969). First, is the belief that the really important affective objectives cannot be attained. The second belief is that any affective objective that can be attained is relatively unimportant.

We have arrived at these beliefs through a natural, but faulty reasoning process. We need to understand this reasoning process. If we can understand this process, it will help us avoid making the same error in the future, as well as provide us with a rationale that will make our affective goals attainable. Below is a four-step example of a teacher involved in the kind of faulty reasoning process that ultimately leads to inaction and the erosion of affective goals.

Step 1.   **We observe the specific behavior of our students.**
          This is, after all, all that we can observe. We cannot see what is going on within them.

4

Mrs. Thompson, the sixth grade teacher, observes Sue's behavior and notices the following:

a. Sue has progressively become more sloppy in her dress and grooming.
b. Sue stays by herself, and will not initiate contact with her classmates. She wanders about waiting to be asked to join in games.
c. Sue often makes negative remarks about herself.
d. Sue made a valid comment in class. Paul disagreed with the comment, and attacked her personally. Sue said nothing.

Step 2. **We infer the existence of a hypothetical construct (an internal entity which has been suggested as existing within us, e.g., self-concept, insecurity, ego, super-ego, etc.).** We do this because we have heard about the hypothetical construct, and recognize that these are the behaviors exhibited by the people with the construct.

Mrs. Thompson infers that Sue has a poor "self-concept."

Step 3. **We develop a circular argument by breathing life into the hypothetical construct.** The hypothetical construct now becomes an internal entity that causes the students to act as they do. At this point, we have concluded that the hypothetical construct really exists, and causes the behaviors. The argument is circular because it involves:

a. observing specific behaviors.
b. inferring the existence of the hypothetical construct based on the behaviors.
c. using the hypothetical construct to explain why the behaviors occurred.

When asked by Mr. Webb, Sue's English teacher, why Sue stays by herself and does not take part in class discussions, Mrs. Thompson declares that it is because she has a poor "self-concept."

Step 4. **We argue for establishing affective goals that required changing the hypothetical construct directly, and depreciate goals involving changing the behaviors from which the hypothetical construct was inferred.**

When discussing Sue with other teachers, Mr. Webb, the English teacher, suggests that they should establish the following educational objectives for Sue:

Sue will:
1. "stand up for her own ideas."
2. "improve her dress and grooming."
3. "initiate contact with her peers."
4. "make positive comments about herself."

In response to Mr. Webb's suggested objectives, Mrs. Thompson replies: "What really needs to be changed is Sue's 'self-concept.' The behaviors that Mr. Webb has suggested we alter are really trivial.

They are only symptomatic of the poor 'self-concept.' Even if we did change those behaviors, the poor 'self-concept' would only manifest itself in new ways. So we really would not have accomplished anything important."

In the situation described above, Mrs. Thompson develops a circular argument which leads her to believe that she understands and can explain the cause of the behavior of the student. She then determines, consciously or unconsciously, that what really needs to be done for the student cannot be done, and that what can be done for the student is inconsequential. This reasoning process leads to inaction, and ultimately to the erosion of the affective goal--that Sue develop a positive "self-concept."

The erosion of our affective goals comes about through a process similar to that illustrated above. We incorporate abstractions or hypothetical constructs into our affective goals. The abstractions or hypothetical constructs cannot be attained directly. There is no way that we can give our students attitudes, values, appreciations, or positive self-images. We recognize that these are very important goals, and we are reluctant to give them up. As a result, when someone suggests that we focus on attaining affective objectives involving specific behaviors, we tend to feel that the objectives are relatively unimportant and only symptomatic of a deeper underlying problem. This leads to a situation in which we state our general affective goals, but do little that is systematic in the way of attaining them.

Planning for the Attainment of Our Affective Goals

The attainment of our affective goals requires that they be integrated into instructional planning, and a systematic effort made to insure their attainment. Unless this effort is made, the goals will continue to erode.

Affective goals are unique in that there is no way that we can choose not to affect them. We can choose not to work toward the attainment of particular cognitive or psychomotor objectives, and as a result have them remain unchanged. However, our failure to integrate our affective goals into instructional planning just leaves them to be affected in a haphazard fashion.

There are three aspects of affective learning that make leaving the goals to be attained in an incidental fashion dangerous. These are:

1. the tendency of an affective learning experience to accompany every cognitive or psychomotor learning experience that we provide.

2. the occurrence of an affective learning experience whenever we respond or fail to respond to spontaneous classroom events.

3. the continual occurrence of competing affective learning experiences in our classrooms.

An affective learning experience accompanies nearly every cognitive or psychomotor learning experience we provide (Dewey, 1938). Attempts at attaining subject matter objectives are accompanied by success or failure experiences. These experiences, in turn, establish learning conditions which directly affect the desire of our students to continue to learn, their attitude toward school, and their feeling about themselves. Learning experiences of this kind should not be ignored. Ignoring them simply leaves the attainment of our affective objectives to chance, and insures that too large a proportion of the affective learning experiences that occur in the classroom will be inconsistent with the attainment of our objectives.

Leaving our affective objectives to be attained in an incidental fashion is dangerous because an affective learning experience is created every time we react or fail to react to spontaneous classroom events. For example, whenever we acknowledge a student who speaks out without first being recognized, ignore a student whose performance surpasses previous performance, or smile or nod when a question is answered correctly, we are providing an affective learning experience which affects the attainment of affective goals. The learning experience that we provide may either promote the attainment of our affective goals or it may strengthen behaviors which are inconsistent with our affective goals. Our task in attaining our affective goals is to insure that each time we react to a classroom event, we are providing a learning experience which strengthens behaviors which are consistent with our goals and reduces behaviors which are inconsistent with them. This requires that the objectives be integrated into our instructional planning, and a conscious effort made to insure that our reaction creates learning experiences that are consistent with the attainment of the objectives.

A third aspect of affective learning that makes leaving affective objectives to be attained in an incidental fashion dangerous is the continual occurrence of competing affective learning experiences. We characteristically initiate and direct all of the cognitive and psychomotor learning experiences that occur in the classroom. This is not true of affective learning experiences. Classmates are continually providing learning experiences which may be either consistent or inconsistent with our affective goals. The peers are providing affective learning experiences which effect the attainment of our affective objectives when they do such things as laugh at the clowning antics of a student, criticize a student who offers an opinion that differs from that of the group, or praise the accomplishments of a class member. As long as our affective goals are left to be attained in an incidental fashion, the peer group will continue to provide large numbers of affective learning experiences which are inconsistent with the attainment of our affective goals. The integration of affective objectives into instructional planning is necessary if we are to find ways of insuring that the affective learning experiences provided by the peers support rather than detract from the attainment of our affective goals.

The attainment of our affective goals requires that the goals be integrated into the curriculum and a systematic approach taken to insure that they are attained. The systematic approach to the attainment of affective goals requires that they be incorporated into the "Model of the Instructional Act" (Tyler, 1953). More specifically, it means we must:

1. specify our broad general affective goals.

2. reduce our broad general affective goals to more specific affective objectives.

3. design learning experiences to lead to the attainment of our objectives.

4. evaluate the attainment of the objectives.

The "model creates the conditions necessary for the systematic improvement of affective instruction. The incorporation of our affective goals into the model insures that affective instruction becomes integrated with cognitive and psychomotor instruction. The process tends to remove affective learning from the realm of incidental learning. In addition, once our broad general affective goals are incorporated into the "model" and reduced to specific affective objectives, they become attainable. We can design learning experiences to lead to the attainment of the specific affective objectives, and we can evaluate the effectiveness of the learning experiences for the attainment of the objectives.

Break up into small groups to discuss and attempt to answer the following questions.

1. Why do educators attribute such importance to the attainment of affective goals?

2. If teachers and administrators attribute so much importance to affective goals, why do we allow them to erode?

3. Give examples of the kind of circular reasoning that tends to occur when we are discussing the attainment of affective goals. What part does circular reasoning play in the erosion of affective goals?

4. Give examples of teacher statements that indicate they are trying to change a hypothetical construct directly. Can this be done? Why or why not?

5. Give examples of teacher statements that indicate they have breathed life into a hypothetical construct--that it has become an entity.

6. What does the process of assigning the blame for student behavior to a hypothetical construct do for us as educators?

7. How were hypothetical constructs derived? What function do they perform? How do they function in explaining and changing behavior?

What is the Function of Our Affective Goals?

The answer to this question is important in the light of the discussion in the first chapter in which it was indicated that affective goals cannot be attained directly. Based on this, we would seem to be justified in wondering why we should specify the goals at all.

The reason for stating our affective goals is because they are necessary if we are to use the "Model of the Instructional Act" to insure a systematic approach to affective instruction. The need for a systematic approach to the attainment of our affective goals is very important because we do not have the option of not affecting the goals. Nearly everything we do affects them in one way or another, and when we do not systematically plan for the attainment of our affective goals, too many of the learning experiences we provide adversely affect the attainment of the goals.

The affective goals function in the model by giving direction to instruction. The construction of affective goals such as the ones below:

Affective Goals for the Entire Class

The students will become more academically motivated.
The students will become better organized.

Affective Goals for Individual Students

Erick will become more independent.
Jennifer will become more assertive.

is important because they help us keep our learning activities focused. Without this direction, our instruction tends to be haphazard and inefficient. This is true regardless of whether our instruction is concerned with verbal skills, numerical skills, motor skills, or affective behavior.

Good affective instruction requires that we specify, and subsequently reduce, our affective goals to specific behaviors in the manner suggested in the following chapter. The specification and reduction of the general goals are necessary if we are to avoid overlooking many of the specific objectives that are most important for the continued growth of our students. Experience has tended to show that when we do not go through the process of stating and reducing our affective goals, we usually end up with large numbers of specific objectives such as:

The students will:

> come to class on time.
> hand in neat, completed assignments.
> raise their hand and wait to be acknowledged before speaking.
> increase the amount of available study time spent studying.

Behaviors such as these are concerned with creating a good learning environment in the classroom by making the students more conforming and obedient. Our attention tends to focus on these behaviors because they are behaviors that directly affect the running of the classroom, and when these behaviors are not performed, it is threatening to us.

The objectives that tend to be overlooked when we fail to go through the process of stating and reducing our affective goals are objectives that would be derived from reducing goals such as:

The students will:

develop a positive self-concept.
become more independent.
enjoy learning.
be able to interact effectively with their peers.
appreciate democratic attitudes and values.

A little thought about how students develop positive self-concepts, become independent, or come to enjoy learning, etc. should make it apparent that students do not evolve these characteristics as a result of doing such things as coming to class on time and raising their hand before speaking. Positive self-concepts develop as students are challenged and successfully meet the challenge; they become independent as a result of establishing and attaining their own goals; and they come to enjoy learning because they are successful at learning tasks. These are the really important goals for which we are striving. They are, however, goals that tend to be overlooked if they are not stated, and subsequently, reduced to affective objectives.

Affective objectives provide us with a rationale for everything we do or do not do in the area of affective instruction. An instructional procedure is performed because we feel that it will lead to the attainment of our affective goal. Similarly, a procedure is not performed if we feel that it is inconsistent with the attainment of our affective goals. In this way, the objectives provide the justification for all of the learning activities we provide.

How Do We Derive Our Affective Goals?

Affective goals, like other general objectives, are derived as we attempt to answer any number of philosophical questions about the purpose of education and the nature of men and women. A complete discussion of all of these questions is beyond the scope of this text. However, an examination of some of the broad questions and the implications that their answers have for affective goals is necessary.

The derivation of the objectives in all domains begins with a consideration of the purpose of education. The question of the purpose of education is a philosophical one which could, and often does, generate some disagreement. There is, however, not as much disagreement as might be expected. For example, we as educators do not disagree too seriously with the notion that the purpose of education is to develop happy, productive citizens.

If we accept the above as the purpose of education, the objectives can be derived by asking the question:

What do people need to become happy, productive citizens?

The answers to this question are also philosophical, and depend to a large extent on the beliefs we have regarding the nature of men and women and their relationship to society. Examples of the way that these beliefs might be translated into affective goals are shown below:

Beliefs Regarding What is Necessary to Become Happy, Productive Citizens	The Resulting Affective Goals
To be happy and productive, men and women must:	The students will:
1. think they are worthwhile persons.	1. develop a positive self-concept.
2. feel they are reaching their potential.	2. become a self-directed learner.
3. be able to deal effectively with everyday problems.	3. become organized and efficient.
4. be able to interact rewardingly with others.	4. be able to interact effectively in social situations.
5. healthy.	5. appreciate physical activity.
6. enjoy beauty.	6. appreciate nature, art, and music.

The list is incomplete. There are many more possible objectives that we could derive from each belief. In addition, there are as many more beliefs that have direct implications for the development of our affective goals.

Generating Our Lists of Affective Goals.

We are good at generating long lists of affective goals. These goals are usually appropriate in that they describe desirable goals which, if attained, would enhance student growth. However, the lists that we generate normally have a good deal of redundancy, and need to be culled to make them more useful. For example, the goals in each of the two lists below have such similar meanings that probably only one of them is needed.

List A: The students will enjoy learning.
The students will like to learn.
The students will be interested in learning.
The students will appreciate learning.
The students will value learning.

List B: The students will develop positive self-concepts.
The students will develop a good self-image.
The students will develop good ego strength.

The terms liking, enjoying, appreciating, valuing, etc. have such a similar meaning that we are talking about essentially the same thing in all of the objectives on list "A". Similarly, "self-concept", "self-image", and "ego strength" refer to similar characteristics so only one of them is needed.

The affective goals that we construct need to be concerned with only one idea if they are to function in the "model", and help us systematically improve our affective instruction. If our goal contains more than one main idea it cannot be reduced easily to specific objectives. A goal which contains two or more ideas which are important should be separated, and a new goal constructed for each idea. For example, the goal:

> The students will develop a respect for individual worth, an understanding of minority opinions, and acceptance of majority decisions.

contains three ideas: 1) the respect for individual worth, 2) an understanding of minority opinions, and 3) an acceptance of majority decisions. Two of the three parts are affective, and the third part is cognitive. If all of the three goals are felt to be important, three new goals should be formed. We should follow a similar procedure with any compound objective that appears on our list.

Practice Exercise 1-2

Form small groups composed of individuals with similar areas of interest. As a group, attempt to derive a list of affective goals that you feel are important, and for which you feel you should strive. After the list has been derived, write statements regarding what each affective goal does for you, and how the goal was derived.

Determining Our Specific Affective Objectives

The second step in incorporating our affective goals into the model of the educational act requires that we reduce our broad, general affective goals to specific objectives. This step is necessary because we cannot attain our broad, general affective goals directly.

The reduction of our broad, general affective goals to specific affective objectives involves the assumption that the additive result of the attainment of our specific affective objectives will be progress toward the attainment of our general goal. Is the assumption justified? It appears to be if we analyze the only options available to us in attempting to develop and use concepts. In the thinking process we observe specific objectives and events, combine them in various ways to form categories, and then use the categories in logical systems. In this process we are forming categories and thinking with them. The process of reducing our broad, general affective goals requires that we move in the opposite direction. It requires that we analyze the categories we have already developed, and determine the specific behaviors that comprise them. Initially, we went from specific behaviors to general concepts. In the reduction process we go from the general concepts to the specific behaviors. It would seem that if we are justified in going from specific to general, we are justified in reversing the process. How well the specific behaviors reflect the general concepts, however, is a function of how we perform the analytic process.

The determination of the specific behaviors that are indicative of the attainment of our broad general affective goals, and the subsequent incorporation of these behaviors into specific affective objectives, do two things that contribute to the systematic improvement of our affective instruction. First, the incorporation of affective objectives containing specific behaviors into the model suggests appropriate learning experiences for the attainment of the objectives. Appropriate learning experiences are suggested because the specific objectives involve increasing or decreasing the frequency or duration with which the students perform rather specific behaviors, and both the kind of learning and the learning conditions necessary for bringing about these behavior changes are known. The second way that the incorporation of the specific objectives into the model leads to the systematic improvement of affective instruction is by making evaluation possible. Once the specific behaviors are determined and incorporated into specific affective objectives, it is possible to evaluate them by counting or timing the increases or decreases in the frequency or duration of their occurrence. Systematic improvement in our affective instruction occurs as we proceed to formulate and test hypotheses regarding the effect that our instructional procedures have on increasing or decreasing the frequency or duration of the specific behaviors.

Determining the Behaviors

The first step in constructing our specific affective objectives is to determine the specific behaviors we feel would provide good evidence that we are attaining our broad general affective goals.

We arrive at these specific behaviors by trying to determine the behaviors that are and are not performed by people who have the general characteristic. The specific behaviors that we derive in this manner will be both positive and negative. The

15

positive behaviors are the desired behaviors that we would like our students to perform with either greater frequency or duration. The negative behaviors are undesired behaviors that the students are performing either too frequently or for too great a duration. These behaviors usually are deemed undesirable because they are incompatible with the performance of the desired positive behaviors (i.e., the individual cannot perform the two behaviors at the same time).

The process of reducing our broad general affective objective to specific objectives begins by asking the question:

> What kinds of things do people do, who have the general characteristics, that others do not do?

The answers to this question provides us with a tentative list of positive behaviors that are thought to provide evidence that the broad general affective objective is being attained. For example, if we have established the broad general affective objective that:

> The students appreciate the dignity and worth of others.

Then, the question we ask to reduce the objective to specific behaviors is:

> What kinds of things do people do, who appreciate the dignity and worth of others, that others do not do?

The answer to the question leads to a list of positive specific behaviors that we feel directly relate to the attainment of the general objective.

The process of generating answers to the question is a creative act. In actuality we are involved in the process of operationally defining the general concepts in terms of behaviors. The generation of the tentative list of behaviors usually takes some time. There are ebbs and flows in the process. However, at this point in the process, we should include nearly any suggested behavior on the list. Our only requirement is that the suggested behavior be rather specific and observable.

The result of our inserting the phrase, "appreciation of the dignity and worth of others," into the general questions might be a list of behaviors such as the ones below:

> Seek peer approval for social isolates in the class.
> Defend others against aggression.
> Defend the right of others to be different.
> Help others.
> Care for the property of others.
> Acknowledge the accomplishments of others.
> Associate with individuals from different ethnic, racial, social, and religious groups.

At this point, our list of behaviors is only tentative.

The positive behaviors that we ultimately incorporate into our specific affective objectives should be 1) behaviors that provide good evidence that our broad general affective goal is being attained, and 2) behaviors that are performed by people who have the general characteristic, and only by people who have the general characteristic. Many of the behaviors that appear on our initial lists may be desirable behaviors, but may not be behaviors that meet the two criteria.

To determine if the behaviors we have suggested provide good evidence of the attainment of the broad general affective goal, we ask the question:

> Are people with general characteristics more likely to perform the behavior than people without the characteristic?

If the behavior we have suggested provides good evidence of the attainment of the broad general goal, the answer to the question should be "yes".

To determine if the behaviors that we have suggested are performed by people who have the general characteristic, and only by people who have the general characteristic, we ask the question:

> Are people, who do not have this general characteristic, also likely to perform this behavior?

Asking this question allows us to eliminate behaviors which, though desirable, are not indicative of the general characteristic stated in the affective goal. If the behavior suggested is performed by people with the general characteristic, and only by people with the general characteristic, the answer to the second question should be "No".

To test the quality of the evidence provided by the behaviors suggested above, we can incorporate each of the behaviors into the two questions in a manner similar to that used below:

> Are people, who appreciate the dignity and worth of others, more likely to seek peer approval for social isolates than someone who does not have the characteristic?

> Are people, who do not appreciate the dignity and worth of others, also likely to seek peer approval for social isolates?

The answers appear to be "Yes" and "No" respectively. The behavior of seeking peer approval for the social isolates in the group appears to provide good evidence of an appreciation of the dignity and worth of others.

The incorporation of the second suggested behavior into the two questions yields a different result. When the questions are asked:

> Are people, who appreciate the dignity and worth of others, more likely to defend others against aggression than people who do not have this characteristic?

> Are people, who do not appreciate the dignity and worth of others, also likely to defend others against aggression?

the answers tend to be "Yes" and "Yes". The behavior fails to satisfy the criterion posed by the second question. People, who do not appreciate the dignity and worth of others, will also defend others against aggression. Gang members defend gang members when they are attacked. However, they do not necessarily appreciate the dignity and worth of others. The suggested behavior could be altered so that it would pass the test posed by the second question. If the behavior were stated, "Defend all others against aggression," the behavior would probably be acceptable.

We do not always have complete agreement about the behaviors that constitute good evidence of the attainment of a broad general objective. The disagreement usually stems from the arbitrary nature of the general concepts that comprise the general affective goals and from the tendency we have to try to determine the motivation behind the specific behaviors. These disagreements need to be resolved. Disagreements that stem from the arbitrary nature of the concepts contained in the general goal can usually be remediated by looking at the way that different authorities define the concept, and then selecting the definition that most nearly fits the meaning we want assigned to our goal. Our tendency to look for the motive behind a behavior also creates a stumbling block to the development of the lists of behaviors. For example, the behavior of discovering real-world applications of mathematical principles might not be accepted as evidence of an appreciation of mathematics. People making this objection usually do so because they feel the behavior is motivated more by the desire for a good grade than an appreciation of mathematics. The point needs to be made that the reason the behavior is performed is unimportant. It is enough that the behavior is performed. Our job as teachers is to find ways of stimulating and strengthening such desired behaviors. If the behaviors can be strengthened enough, they will become self-reinforcing. For our purposes in constructing specific affective objectives, the emphasis must be on the quality of the evidence provided by the behavior--not on the motivation behind the behavior.

We usually have little trouble arriving at the negative behaviors that we desire to reduce or eliminate. These are behaviors that directly or indirectly interfere with the attainment of our positive goals. The behaviors characteristically are concerned with classroom management. For example, they are concerned with reducing or eliminating such student behaviors as coming to class late, clowning, failing to do assignments, disrupting the class, talking back to the teacher, etc. The reason we are so adept at deriving these negative behaviors is because they are so apparent. These behaviors pose a threat to us because they interfere both with the development of a smooth running classroom and with the attainment of our positive goals.

There is a danger that our affective instruction will come to focus on behaviors related to classroom management rather than on behaviors more directly concerned with student growth. This situation is most likely to occur when we skip the steps of stating and reducing our general affective objectives. For example, when we are given an individual case study or descriptions of classroom occurrences, our tendency is to focus on the elimination of disruptive behaviors and the strengthening of behaviors consistent with a smooth running classroom. This is a beneficial process, and probably explains the disciplinary emphasis found in many behavior modification programs. However, when we utilize this approach exclusively, and fail to state and systematically reduce our broad general affective goals, we are in danger of directing our affective instruction toward creating conforming and obedient students rather than promoting their intellectual and psychological growth.

Developing Our Affective Objectives

The positive and negative behaviors we derive as a result of the above process can be incorporated into specific affective objectives and used in the "model" to improve affective instruction.

18

Our specific affective objectives differ in two important ways from specific objectives in the cognitive and psychomotor domains. First, the specific affective objectives are concerned primarily with increasing or decreasing the frequency or duration of voluntary behaviors that are already in the repertoire of the students. Second, the specific affective objectives tend to come in pairs involving both a positive and a negative objective.

The specific affective objectives that we derive have six characteristics. These are:

They are written in terms of changes that are to occur in student behavior.
They are concerned with "will do" rather than "can do."
They are often constructed in pairs with a positive and a negative objective.
They have a main verb that is observable.

The behavior involved is relatively specific.
The way to evaluate the attainment of the objective is apparent.

Below are two specific affective objectives that meet the six criteria suggested above.

> The students will increase the duration of available study time spent studying.

> The students will reduce the amount of available study time spent wandering about the room.

The emphasis in the two objectives above is on changing the behavior of the students. Notice that in the objectives the teachers do not indicate what they are going to do for the students, but rather what the students are to do.

The two specific affective objectives are concerned with increasing the frequency or duration of the performance of voluntary behaviors that the students can already perform. For this reason the emphasis in the objectives is on "Will do" rather than "Can do." The objectives necessarily involve the assumption that the students have the ability to perform the behaviors. The students have the physical capability of increasing studying and reducing wandering behavior. The objective is not to teach the students how to study, but to increase the amount of time spent studying.

The objectives are paired. The first objective is positive because it is concerned with increasing the desirable behavior of studying. The second objective is negative because it is concerned with decreasing the undesirable behavior of wandering about the room. The reason it is often necessary to write the objectives in pairs is because attaining the positive objective often requires a corresponding reduction in the negative behavior. We need two objectives because we need two learning experiences to attain our positive goal. In the case of these objectives we need to design learning experiences both for strengthening studying behavior and to reducing wandering behavior. We will never be very successful in strengthening studying behavior if the behavior of wandering about the room remains strong.

The main verb in both objectives is observable. The behaviors of studying and wandering about the room can be seen. The quality of observability is necessary if the objectives are to be evaluated.

The behaviors of studying and wandering about the room are rather specific. There is more than one way of studying and probably several ways of wandering about the room. However, the behaviors appear to be specific enough to perform in the model. Behaviors can always be reduced further. So the question becomes how specific must the behaviors be before they can function in an objective. The answer seems to be that the behaviors should be specific enough so that they can function as a guideline for teacher action. It should be specific enough so that the teacher standing in front of the class can observe it, determine that it is or is not the desired behavior, and act to strengthen or weaken it.

Finally, if the objective is constructed properly, there should be little question about how to evaluate its attainment. The first objective can be evaluated by determining the amount of available study time spent studying before and after the learning experiences. Wandering behavior can be evaluated in the same way. Nearly all of the specific affective objectives we desire to attain can be evaluated by either timing or counting the changes that occur in the behaviors before and after the learning experience.

Examples of Our Affective Objectives

The number and kinds of specific affective objectives with which we are concerned vary depending upon the age of our students and the subject matter that we teach. Below are a number of broad, general affective objectives and the specific affective objectives derived from them. The examples are presented to give some idea of the kinds of specific affective objectives of concern to teachers. The positive objectives contain desirable behavior that should be strengthened. The negative objectives contain undesired behaviors which need to be reduced or eliminated before we can hope to be successful in strengthening the positive behaviors. The lists are not intended to be complete, but rather to illustrate the results of the reduction process and the nature of specific affective objectives.

In examining these lists, two things should be noted. First, we should note that there is not always a negative objective for each positive objective. The negative objectives are only necessary when there are specific undesirable behaviors that are incompatible with increasing the desired behavior stated in the positive objectives. The second thing that should be noted is that we can have affective objectives concerned with cognitive behaviors. For example, listed under the broad general affective objective concerned with the appreciation of literature are specific objectives indicating that the students will increase the frequencies with which they draw inferences from literature to life, compare characters from different literary compositions, and infer the motives of the characters. Each of these objectives is concerned with increasing the frequencies with which a cognitive behavior is performed. The objectives, however, are affective because they are concerned with increasing the frequency of the behavior, not with teaching the students how to perform the behaviors. The learning experiences necessary to strengthen the behaviors are quite different from the learning experiences necessary for teaching the students how to perform the behaviors. We clearly have no assurance that because students have been taught how to perform a behavior they will perform it with the needed frequency or duration.

The broad, general affective objective--The students will become responsible class members:

Positive specific affective objectives—The students will increase the frequency and/or duration with which they:

come to class on time.
bring books and materials to class.
have their assignments done neatly.
have their assignments done on time.
attempt to take part in class discussions.
ask relevant questions.

Negative specific affective objectives—The students will decrease the frequency and/or duration with which they:

are late for class.
fail to bring books and materials to class.
hand in sloppy assignments.
hand their assignments in late.
fail to take part in class discussions.
pester their classmates during study time.
fail to ask questions.

The broad, general affective objective—<u>The students will become organized learners</u>:

Positive specific affective objectives—The students will increase the frequency and/or duration with which they:

write down their assignments.
establish long-term goals for themselves.
plan their day.
follow the plan.
prioritize their plan.
modify their plan.
accomplish their plan.

Negative specific affective objectives—The students will decrease the frequency and/or duration with which they:

state that they could not remember the assignment.
exhibit non-goal directed behavior.
fail to establish goals.
establish inappropriate goals.

The broad, general affective objective—<u>The students will appreciate the dignity and worth of others</u>:

Positive specific affective objectives—The students will increase the frequency and/or duration with which they:

seek peer acceptance of the social isolates within the class.
defend others against aggression.
defend the right of others to be different.
acknowledge the accomplishments of others.
help less able students.
attempt to include social isolates in group activities.

Negative specific affective objectives--The students will decrease the frequency and/or duration with which they:

ridicule the social isolates within the class.
encourage conflict between members of different groups.
are critical of those who deviate from group standards.
belittle the accomplishments of others.
ignore less able students.
ignore social isolates.

The broad, general affective objective--The students will develop a feeling of self-worth:

Positive specific affective objectives--The students will increase the frequency and/or duration with which they:

offer their opinions even when those opinions differ from that of the group.
defend themselves against aggression.
seek out new challenges.
establish their own goals.
make their own decisions.
push to attain their own goals.

Negative specific affective objectives--The students will decrease the frequency and/or duration with which they:

alter their opinions so that they conform to that of the group.
fail to respond when they are the subject of verbal or physical aggression.
avoid taking part in new activities.
modify their goals to conform to group goals.
ask others to make their decisions for them.
fail to push for the attainment of their own goal.

The broad, general affective objective--The students will appreciate literature:

The students will increase the frequency and/or duration with which they:

read literature.
draw inferences from literature to life.
compare characters from different literary compositions.
discuss a character or situation in a story.
imitate the writing of the author.
compare the method and style of authors.
determine the motives of the characters.

The broad, general affective objective--The students will appreciate nature:

The students will increase the frequency with which they:

attempt to grow things.
read about environmental problems.
participate in attempts to clean up rivers and streams.
attempt to evaluate arguments regarding pollution control.
are politically active concerning environmental problems.
discuss the balances that exist in nature.
practice conservation measures.

The students will decrease the frequency and/or duration with which they:

utilize practices that are wasteful of natural resources.
litter.
damage wildlife, flora and fauna.
make indiscriminant use of insect and rodent poisons.
disconnect the pollution control devices on their cars.

There are many other broad, general affective objectives that are of concern to us. Some of the goals are of concern to all teachers, and some are of concern to teachers in specific subject matter areas. We need to take the time to think about our affective goals, and then reduce them to specific affective objectives. When this is done, our objectives will be able to guide our learning experiences, and their attainment will no longer be left to chance.

Summary

We consider the attainment of affective goals very important. The goals occupy dominant positions in nearly every statement of the goals and purposes that we construct. Closer observation, however, reveals the affective goals that are present during initial planning tend to erode. The erosion is evident because few learning experiences are provided specifically to lead to the attainment of the objectives, and there is seldom any evaluation of the extent to which the objectives are attained.

A primary reason for the erosion of our affective goals stems from our tendency to assign causality to hypothetical constructs. We have come to believe that these constructs are the causes of our behaviors. The problem arises because we cannot change the hypothetical construct directly. We recognize that we can change the behaviors. However, we believe that these are only symptomatic of the real problem-- the hypothetical construct, and for this reason we have come to believe that changing the specific behaviors is unimportant. The result is a tendency to state broad, general affective goals, but to do nothing to lead to their attainment.

The erosion of our affective goals has left them to be affected in an incidental fashion. This has serious consequences because everything we do or do not do affects the attainment of the goals in one way or another. Affective learning experiences are likely to accompany every cognitive or psychomotor learning experience we provide. In addition, an affective learning experience is likely to occur whenever we react or fail to react to a classroom event. The problem that occurs when affective instruction is left incidental to the instructional process is too many affective learning experiences are provided that are incompatible with the attainment of our desired affective goals.

Our affective instruction needs to be planned and carried out in a systematic fashion. This can be done by using the "Model of the Instructional Act." The use of the model systematizes affective instruction by requiring us to state our affective goals, reduce them to specific affective objectives, design learning experiences to lead to the attainment of the objectives, and evaluate them to determine whether or not the objectives have been attained. The result of this approach is to remove affective instruction from the realm of incidental instruction and place it in the realm of planned instruction.

Affective goals are derived from our beliefs regarding the purpose of education, the nature of men and women and their relationship to society.

Affective goals are necessary for a systematic approach to affective instruction. The general affective goals function in the model by giving direction to the instructional process. Without them, affective instruction tends to be haphazard, creating a situation where too many of our learning experiences are inconsistent with our desired goals.

The affective goals must be stated and then systematically reduced to specific affective objectives, if we are to avoid overlooking many of the objectives that are most important to the continued growth of our students. If the affective goals are not systematically reduced, affective instruction tends to focus on objectives concerned with classroom management rather than objectives that are more directly concerned with student growth.

The second step in affective instruction is incorporating our affective goals into the model of the educational act. This requires the reduction of the broad, general affective goals into specific affective objectives. This process is necessary because the affective goals cannot be attained directly.

The incorporation of the specific affective objectives into the model contributes to the systematic improvement of affective instructions both by suggesting appropriate learning experiences and by making evaluation possible. Once the specific objectives are incorporated into the model, we can systematically formulate and test hypotheses to determine the learning experiences that are most effective for attaining the objectives. This process makes a systematic approach to affective instruction possible.

The behaviors to be incorporated into the specific objectives are derived through an analytical process by asking the question: "What kinds of things do people do who have the general characteristic that others do not do?" The resulting behaviors must then be analyzed to determine if they are behaviors performed by people with the general characteristic, and only by people with the general characteristic.

The specific behaviors that result from reducing the affective goals must be incorporated into specific affective objectives with the following characteristics if they are to function in the model. They are:

> be stated in terms of student behaviors.
> be directional.
> be concerned with "will do" rather than "can do."
> have an observable main verb.
> describe a relatively specific behavior.
> be readily evaluated.

Get together with a small group who has the same general area of interest. Listed below are three affective goals that are thought to be important.

1. The students will become self-disciplined.
2. The students will become self-directed learners.
3. The students will appreciate democratic attitudes and values.

Either select one of the three affective goals above or develop your own affective goal, and attempt to develop the specific affective objectives related to it. Write your affective goal below.

After you have listed the affective goal, attempt to derive a list of appropriate behaviors by asking the question:

What .... do?

Check the behaviors above to determine that they are performed by people, who have the general characteristic described in your affective goal, and only by people with the general characteristic. Do this by asking the questions:

Are people, who have the general characteristic, more likely
to perform the behaviors than someone who does not have it?

Are people who do not have the general characteristic, also
likely to perform the behaviors?

The answers to the two questions should be "yes" and "no" respectively. If they are not, the behavior should be either eliminated or modified so there is general agreement that the answers are "yes" and "no". Write "yes" or "no" after the behaviors as you ask each question.

Construct specific affective objectives using the behaviors derived above:

1.

2.

3.

4.

5.

6.

7.

8.

Check your specific behavioral objectives to see that they meet the six criteria below. If they do not meet the criteria, try to modify them so that they do. Make sure your objectives:

1. are written in terms of changes to occur in the behavior of the students.
2. are directional indicating a desire to increase or decrease the frequency and/or duration of the behavior.
3. are concerned with "Will do" rather than "Can do."
4. have an observable main "verb."
5. describe a behavior that is relatively specific.
6. can be readily evaluated.

References

Bandura, A. (1969). Principles of behavior modification. New York: Holt, Rinehart and Winston.

Dewey, J. (1938). Experiences and education. New York: Macmillan.

Krathwohl, D. R. (1964). The taxonomy of educational objectives: Affective domain. New York: David McKay.

Spears, H. (1973). Kappans ponder the goals of education. Phi Delta Kappan, 55, 29-32.

Tyler, R. (1951). The function of measurement in improving instruction. In E. F. Lindquist (Ed.), Educational measurement (pp. 47-67). Menasha, WI: George Banta Publishing Co.

Chapter 2

SIGNAL LEARNING AND OUR AFFECTIVE INSTRUCTION

Behavioral Objectives for Chapter 2

When you have completed this chapter you should be able to:

1. recognize what is learned in signal learning.

2. identify examples of signal learning.

3. identify examples and characteristics of signal learning responses.

4. identify characteristics and examples of unconditioned stimuli.

5. identify characteristics and examples of conditioned stimuli.

6. recognize the sequence of elements in a signal learning episode.

7. recognize what constitutes reasonable evidence that signal learning has occurred.

8. identify examples of conditioned aversive stimuli.

9. recognize how anxiety becomes associated with a particular stimuli.

10. recognize the conditions necessary for something to become a positive conditioned stimulus.

11. recognize the effect of contiguity on signal learning.

12. recognize the effects of anxiety and intelligence on signal learning.

13. recognize the effect of repetition in signal learning.

14. recognize the effect of motivation on signal learning.

15. identify the conditions under which one trial signal learning may occur.

16. identify examples of stimulus generalization.

17. identify examples and characteristics of stimulus generalization.

18. recognize the effects of practice on stimulus discrimination.

19. identify examples of incidental learning.

20. define and identify new examples of forgetting.

21. define and identify new examples of extinction.

22. define and identify new examples of reconditioning.

23. given classroom situations, recognize the manner in which signal learning is likely to occur.

24. given classroom situations, identify the signal learning experiences to which different students are exposed.

25. recognize the relationship of grades to signal learning.

26. given classroom situations, recognize how negative signal learning affects the attainment of cognitive and psychomotor objectives.

27. recognize how grades function in signal learning episodes.

28. recognize the affective dilemma that teachers face in attempting to attain their cognitive objectives.

29. given classroom situations, recognize the teacher's task when students exhibit a high degree of anxiety.

30. recognize those things most likely to function as unconditioned stimuli in the classroom.

31. recognize the characteristics of signal learning that make it important in the classroom.

Discovering the Problem

Get together in small groups to discuss the situation below and answer the questions that follow. The affective goal of Mrs. Ewald is that her students like to read. Tony is the youngest boy in her first grade class. He is not ready to read. He tends to reverse words like "was" and "saw;" and he cannot learn the rules of phonics. However, because reading is taught in the first grade, Mrs. Ewald has to attempt to teach him to read. She attempts to do this by the "look-say" method in which he is required to recognize each word by sight. During reading instruction, Tony is required to read aloud. He makes many errors, and has been placed in the slow reading group. Is Mrs. Ewald providing a learning experience that affects the attainment of her affective goal? If so, how does this learning experience occur? Did Mrs. Ewald actually plan to provide a learning experience to effect the attainment of her affective goal? What kind of a learning experience has Mrs. Ewald actually planned to provide? What should she have done? If Tony had done very well in reading would Mrs. Ewald be providing a learning experience that affected the attainment of her affective goal?

The Importance of Signal Learning to Affective Instruction

The third step in the affective instructional process is the designing of learning experiences for our students. We have two types of learning that directly or indirectly affect the attainment of our affective goals. These are signal learning or classical conditioning and operant learning (Gagne, 1985). The two types of learning are quite different. They differ both in the conditions necessary for the learning to take place, and the effect that the learning has on the learners. The current chapter is concerned with signal learning.

Signal learning differs from other kinds of learning because although it occurs, and indirectly affects the attainment of our objectives, it does not function in the model of the educational act. It does not function because we cannot construct specific affective objectives that can be attained directly through the use of signal learning, and we typically cannot evaluate signal learning outcomes in the classroom.

Signal learning or classical conditioning is an important type of learning for affective instruction (Ringness, 1975). It is through signal learning that our students develop their emotional responses to school, teachers, subject matter, learning, reading, and all the other objects and activities associated with the learning process. The signal learning experiences to which we expose our students can be either positive or negative. If the signal learning experiences that our students have related to school activities are positive, they tend to develop positive emotional responses to the activities. Students, who have positive signal learning experiences associated with school-related activities, come to enjoy the activities and seek them out. They like school, and they value the learning activities that go on in the school. This is not true of students who primarily have negative signal learning experiences associated with school. For these students, school and school-related activities tend to elicit the negative emotional responses of fear and anxiety. These students when exposed to the learning activities of the school tend to try to escape or withdraw rather than actively participate in them.

The Nature of Signal Learning

Signal learning is also called classical conditioning. It is the type of learning through which an involuntary, imprecise, emotional response becomes associated with a stimulus that previously did not elicit the response.

The two classic experiments that are examples of signal learning are those performed by Pavlov (1927) and Watson and Raynor (1920). These two experiments are used below to illustrate the conditions necessary for signal learning to occur.

In the Pavlov experiment dogs were taught to salivate at the sound of a buzzer. He did this by arranging a sequence in which the dog heard a buzzer, and was then fed. He found that after the sequence was repeated a number of times, the dogs began to salivate every time the buzzer was sounded. They did this in the absence of food. The signal learning sequence can be diagrammed as follows:

```
1.  Buzzer          Food----------Salivating
    Sc              Su                 R


2.  Buzzer---------------Salivating
    Sc                        R
```

The first line above shows the conditions necessary for signal learning to occur. The second line indicates that the signal learning has been completed, and that the buzzer is able to cause salivating without the presence of food.

There are three components to a signal learning episode. These are the conditioned stimulus, the unconditioned stimulus and the response. The conditioned stimulus, the "Sc" in the diagram above, is the stimulus which was not able to elicit the response prior to the occurrence of signal learning. In the Pavlov experiment this was the buzzer. Buzzers normally do not cause dogs to salivate. The unconditioned stimulus, the "Su" in the diagram, is a stimulus which is capable of eliciting the response without any learning. The "Su" in the experiment above was the food. Dogs do not have to learn to salivate when they are presented with food. It occurs naturally. The third component of a signal learning episode is the response. It should be noted that in signal learning no new response is learned. In this way signal learning differs from most other kinds of learning. The response which is involuntary, imprecise and uncontrolled is already in the repertoire of the learner (i.e., the dogs were already able to salivate before the Pavlov experiment). What was learned was a new connection. A stimulus, which had not been able to cause the involuntary, imprecise, uncontrolled response of salivating, became able to elicit it after the learning.

The Watson experiment can be used to illustrate signal learning in a human subject. In this experiment Watson used a little boy named Albert and a white rabbit. He first established that Albert liked the white rabbit. He then arranged a sequence of events in which the presentation of the white rabbit was immediately followed by a loud noise. Signal learning occurred. This was demonstrated by the fact that the previously neutral or perhaps positive stimulus, the white rabbit, came to elicit in Albert the involuntary, imprecise, emotional response of fear or anxiety.

The External Conditions for Signal Learning

The conditions necessary for signal learning to occur have been well established by many experiments (Kimble, 1967). For signal learning to occur the components must occur in the right order. The conditioned stimulus must be presented and followed closely by the unconditioned stimulus. The learning will not occur if the order is reversed. For signal learning to occur in the Watson experiment the conditioned stimulus, the white rabbit, had to be followed by the unconditioned stimulus, the loud noise. Presenting the loud noise, and then the rabbit, would not cause the learning to occur.

There need be no similarity between the conditioned stimulus and the unconditioned stimulus for signal learning to occur. There was no stimulus similarity between the buzzer and the food in the Pavlov experiment or between the rabbit and the loud noise in the Watson experiment. All that was needed for the learning to occur was a time sequence in which the conditioned stimulus was followed almost immediately by an unconditioned stimulus.

In reality, signal learning, as it occurs in the everyday world, appears to require only the presentation of an unconditioned stimulus. When the unconditioned stimulus is presented, whatever the learner was focused upon immediately prior to the presentation of the unconditioned stimulus tends to become a conditioned stimulus. For this reason every act of punishment or reward tends to create the conditions necessary for signal learning to occur. The attention of the learner is always focused on something immediately prior to being punished or rewarded, and because there need be no stimulus similarity between the conditioned stimulus and the unconditioned stimulus, these stimuli tend to come to evoke either positive or negative emotional responses from the learner.

Signal learning does not have to occur every time a stimulus is followed by an unconditioned stimulus. Whether signal learning occurs or not depends on the strength of the unconditioned stimulus. If the presentation of the unconditioned stimulus is traumatic enough, one trial learning tends to occur. Watson apparently attained one trial learning with little Albert and the white rabbit. The probability of signal learning occurring, and the conditioned stimulus coming to elicit the same response as the unconditioned stimulus, apparently increases or decreases with the degree of the perceived punishment or reward attached to the unconditioned stimulus.

Signal learning also results in stimulus generalization. Stimulus generalization occurs when not only the conditioned stimulus comes to elicit the response, but other stimuli that are similar in appearance to the original stimulus also come to elicit the response. In the Watson experiment not only the white rabbit, but small white animals in general came to elicit fear and anxiety. Little Albert not only was afraid of white rabbits, but white cats and dogs. Through stimulus generalization the emotional responses of the learner come to be elicited by many other objects that are in some way similar to the conditioned stimulus involved in the signal learning experience. In his way, they too become conditioned stimuli.

Repetition of the signal learning episodes tends to reduce stimulus generalization and increase stimulus discrimination. The Watson experiment can also be used to illustrate this relationship. If the signal learning sequence-white rabbit, loud noise, is repeated often enough, little Albert will begin to discriminate that it is only the white rabbit and not other white animals that is followed by the loud noise. After this discrimination is made, only the presentation of the white rabbit will be followed by fear and anxiety.

The signal learning connection, once it is established, tends to be retained over extended periods of time. Those stimuli that become paired in the mind of the learner with either a positive emotional response or fear and anxiety tend to keep on eliciting these responses. The connections, however, may be "forgotten" if the learner is placed in a situation in which the conditioned stimulus is not presented over an extended period of time.

Signal learning connections, even though they are very resistant to forgetting, can be broken or altered through the processes of "extinction" and "reconditioning."

Extinction of signal learning connections occurs when the conditioned stimulus is continually presented, but is not followed by the unconditioned stimulus. For example, if in the Watson experiment, the "Sc", the white rabbit, were presented over and over again without the loud noise, the rabbit would cease to cause Albert anxiety. The connection between the white rabbit and anxiety or fear would have been extinguished. Consistency is an important factor in extinguishing a signal learning connection. The unconditioned stimulus must not be allowed to follow the conditioned stimulus during the process of extinction. If the loud noise is ever allowed to follow the presentation of the white rabbit the extinction of the rabbit-anxiety connection will be much more difficult.

Reconditioning is the procedure that is most often used to break the connection between a conditioned stimulus and a response. This is because reconditioning is a more efficient process than extinction. Reconditioning occurs when the original signal learning sequence is altered so that the conditioned stimulus is followed almost immediately by an unconditioned stimulus that elicits the opposite response from that used during the initial learning experience. For example, Watson performed a second experiment that involved the reconditioning of Albert. After causing the white rabbit to become a conditioned stimulus that elicited fear and anxiety from Albert, Watson reconditioned him by exposing him to the following signal learning episode:

1. white rabbit   food   positive emotional response
        Sc   Su ----------------R

2. white rabbit   positive emotional response
        Sc ------------------------R

The reconditioning experiment was performed by putting the white rabbit in the doorway some distance away from Albert, and then feeding Albert. This procedure was followed a number of times with the rabbit being brought a little closer to Albert each time. As a result, Albert was soon playing with the rabbit.

The Internal Conditions and Signal Learning

Individual differences appear to exist in the degree to which individuals tend to be affected by signal learning episodes. The characteristic that seems to have the greatest effect is the anxiety level of the learners. The more anxious the learners, the more readily they can be conditioned. There does not seem to be any relationship between intelligence and the speed with which conditioning occurs.

Motivation, a second internal factor, plays no part in signal learning. This is an important fact, and one that has important implications for us as classroom teachers. Motivation is an important consideration in every other kind of learning, but not for signal learning. An individual can not keep from being conditioned. All that is necessary for signal learning to occur is for a conditioned stimulus to be followed by an unconditioned stimulus of the appropriate strength or with the necessary frequency. The motivation or intent of the learner is not a factor. The response involved in signal learning is an involuntary response, and the learner cannot keep the connection between the new stimulus and the involuntary response from being established.

34

Practice Exercise 2-1

1. What is learned in signal learning?

2. List the three components of signal learning.

3. Describe the characteristics of an unconditioned stimulus.

4. Describe the nature of the signal learning response.

5. What things can become conditioned stimuli?

6. Diagram the conditions necessary for signal learning to occur.

7. Construct a diagram that indicates that signal learning has occurred.

8. Why is the presentation of an unconditioned stimulus all that is   necessary for signal learning to occur?

9. What things present in the school environment have come to function   as unconditioned stimuli? How did this occur?

10. What part does motivation play in signal learning?

11. Describe the conditions necessary for breaking the connection between learning activities and anxiety. What are the processes called?

Using and Controlling Signal Learning in Our Schools

Signal learning affects nearly everything we do in the schools. It is the process through which our students come to like or dislike school, teachers, other students, subject matter, and learning.

The importance that signal learning has in the schools is attributable to a combination of factors.

The first factor that contributes to the importance of signal learning in the schools is the fact that motivation plays no part in signal learning. Our students cannot determine that they will or will not be conditioned. The learning occurs regardless of the intent of the learner. This is a characteristic of signal learning that differs from most of the other kinds of learning that go on in the school. Our students can evaluate most of the learning tasks that they are given, and based on this evaluation, make decisions whether or not to learn the material. They can choose not to learn the various aspects of English, mathematics, science, or social studies. Intent, however, is not a factor in determining whether or not signal learning occurs.

A second factor that makes signal learning important in the schools stems from the fact that all that is necessary for signal learning to occur is the presentation of an unconditioned stimulus. This is because something always precedes the presentation of the unconditioned stimulus; and whatever our students are focused upon immediately prior to the presentation of the unconditioned stimulus tends to become a conditioned stimulus. Thus, the presentation of the unconditioned stimulus completes the temporal conditions necessary for signal learning to occur. This can be illustrated by placing the conditions described above in the signal learning diagram as follows:

	Focus of	Positive or Negative Unconditioned	Positive or Negative Emotional
1.	Attention	Stimulus	Response
	Sc	Su--------------------R	

If the signal learning sequence above is repeated with the necessary frequency, or if the unconditioned stimulus is powerful enough, the signal learning episode goes to completion as shown below:

	Focus of	Positive or Negative Emotional
2.	Attention	Response
	Sc -----------------R	

The third factor that makes signal learning so important in the schools is the fact that a signal learning experience tends to accompany any activity that involves either success of failure. The signal learning experience occurs because most of the indicators of success and failure that we use in the schools have come to function as unconditioned stimuli. Strictly speaking, an unconditioned stimulus is a stimulus that is capable of causing the involuntary, imprecise, emotional response without any learning. However, we now have ample evidence that any stimulus that is continually paired with an unconditioned stimulus can come to function as an unconditioned stimulus. Examples of some of the conditioned stimuli that have come to function as unconditioned stimuli are criticism, praise, some rewards, and grades. Criticism and praise are only words, and would not elicit the emotional response that they do if they had not so often been paired with other kinds of punishment and reward. Many rewards such as money only elicit positive emotional responses because they have been paired with positive unconditioned stimuli such as food and enjoyable activities. The grades that we give are also examples of conditioned stimuli that have come to function as unconditioned stimulus. Our grades are indicators of success or failure, and as such have continually been associated with the unconditioned stimuli of punishment and reward.

The three factors mentioned above combine to ensure that signal learning episodes are going on within the schools all of the time. Any teacher, student, subject matter area, or learning activity that is followed by good grades, praise, recognition, or reward tends to become a positive conditioned stimulus; and conversely, any teacher, student, subject matter area, or learning activity that is followed by low grades, criticism and punishment tends to become a negative conditioned stimulus.

Good grades, praise, recognition, and reward, as well as criticism, bad grades, and punishment are the unconditioned stimuli that give rise to the signal learning episodes that occur in the schools. Nearly everything that goes on in the school is evaluated, and some measure of success or failure attributed to it. The students, who are successful in activities such as reading, mathematics, science experiments, etc., have positive signal learning experiences such as the one diagrammed for reading below. These students tend to come to enjoy the activities and to seek them out.

```
                         Praise          Positive
                         Good grades     Emotional
1.   Reading             Reward          Response
                            Su -----------------R


                         Positive
                         Emotional
2.   Reading             Response
     Sc ---------------------------R
```

Conversely, students who are unsuccessful in these activities have negative signal learning experiences. Their learning experience can be represented by the diagram of a signal learning experience such as the one involving mathematics below:

```
                         Criticism
                         Low grades
1.   Mathematics         Punishment      Anxiety
     Sc                     Su -----------------R

2.   Mathematics         Anxiety
     Sc ----------------------- R
```

37

For students experiencing this signal learning episode, mathematics tends to become a conditioned aversive stimulus that causes anxiety. These students quickly learn to avoid mathematics and anything they associate with it.

Signal learning creates a dilemma for us. The dilemma arises because different students are exposed to different signal learning experience with each cognitive or psychomotor lesson. For successful students the indicators of success, the positive unconditioned stimuli of good grades, praise, recognition, and reward typically accompany the lesson. This is not true for unsuccessful students. For these students the lesson is followed by the indicators of failure. The unconditioned stimuli of criticism, poor grades and punishment, characteristically, accompany the lesson. The result is that the successful students generally tend to enjoy the activity, and those things that they associate with it. While on the other hand, the unsuccessful students come to fear and avoid the activity, and those things they associate with it. The dilemma occurs because in the process of attempting to attain our cognitive and psychomotor objectives we often are providing negative signal learning experiences for those students who are most in need of positive signal learning experiences to reduce their fear and anxiety, and increase their willingness to attend to the learning tasks.

Signal Learning and the Attainment
of Our Affective Objectives

The relationship of signal learning to the attainment of affective objectives differs from the relationship that the other kinds of learning have to the attainment of educational objectives. It is possible to incorporate all of the other kinds of learning into the "Model" of the educational act. We can specify our objective, design learning experiences to lead to the attainment of our objective and evaluate to determine whether or not our objective has been attained. This is not possible with signal learning primarily because the involuntary, imprecise, uncontrolled response involved in signal learning cannot be measured by the devices available to us in the classroom. Yet, we know that signal learning exists; that it is constantly occurring in the classroom; and that it vitally affects the attainment of all kinds of educational objectives. Signal learning cannot be ignored just because its results cannot be measured directly and do not fit nicely into an instructional model.

Signal learning is the only kind of learning that appears to affect the attainment of the broad, general affective objectives directly. This is because both the broad, general affective objectives and signal learning involve the attachment of emotional responses to objects and activities. In constructing our broad, general affective objectives, we indicate that we want our students to do such things as:

 like school.
 be interested in English, mathematics, and science.
 enjoy reading and physical activities.
 appreciate art and music.

When we speak in general terms, our language tends to become imprecise. "Liking", and "being interested in", "enjoying" and "appreciating" are imprecise terms, and it is not clear that they have different meanings. When incorporated into objectives, these words seem to indicate that we desire that a positive emotional response be associated with the particular object or activity. Positive emotional responses are, of course, the kinds of response transferred through signal learning.

Signal learning affects the attainment of broad, general affective objectives of teachers in either a positive or a negative way. These learning experiences go on with or without our planning. Schools, teachers, and activities that are followed by positive unconditioned stimuli tend to be liked, enjoyed, appreciated, and valued; while those that are followed by aversive unconditioned stimuli tend to be disliked, hated, and scorned.

Signal learning generally affects the attainment of cognitive and psychomotor objectives by affecting the willingness of the learner to become involved in the activity. However, it is also true that if the signal learning experiences result in enough anxiety, this anxiety can interfere with the accomplishment of the learning task. The high anxiety that becomes associated with the task tends to limit the flexibility the students exhibit in both learning and problem solving. The result is a tendency on the part of the learners to repeat inappropriate responses rather than try new and different approaches to the tasks.

Signal learning currently exists in the schools as a form of incidental learning. It is incidental learning because even though signal learning experiences accompany nearly every cognitive or psychomotor learning experience that takes place in the schools, we normally do not consider signal learning in our instructional planning. The focus of the planning, instruction, and subsequent evaluation is on the cognitive and psychomotor aspects of instruction while the accompanying signal learning experiences are left to occur in a more or less random fashion. The result of leaving signal learning incidental to the instructional process is the occurrence of far too many negative signal learning experiences. These experiences tend to cause students to dislike and avoid learning activities that are important to their continued growth.

The effective attainment of the affective, cognitive, and psychomotor objectives of the schools requires that signal learning be removed from the realm of incidental learning, and become directly incorporated into our planning and instruction. We need to consider seriously the aversive unconditioned stimuli that tend to follow the learning activities that go on in the school, and take action to see that these stimuli are removed or eliminated. In addition, we need to actively plan learning experiences in which learning activities are followed by positive unconditioned stimuli which will tend to cause them to elicit positive emotional responses from the students.

The Rules for Using Signal Learning in the Classroom

There are a number of things we can do in attempting to insure that our students are exposed primarily to positive rather than negative signal learning experiences in our classroom. These have been incorporated into a series of rules which are listed below.

Rule 1: **Work toward individualizing instruction so that students are given educational objectives to attain that are appropriate for them.**

Avoiding negative signal learning experiences and promoting positive signal learning experiences in the classroom require that we work toward the individualization of instruction. The individualization of instruction is necessary because of the high degree of individual differences that is found in every classroom. Cook (1948) provided information that illustrates the extent of individual differences found in a typical classroom. He pointed out that at the time a random group of six-year-olds enters the first grade a four year mental age span already exists. If the upper and lower 2 percent of the students are disregarded, the lower scoring students have a mental age of four and the higher scoring students have a mental age of eight. These individual differences increase with age. The same group of children will exhibit an eight-year difference in general ability when they are in the sixth grade. The sixth grade class will contain some students who are functioning at the second grade level and have mental age of eight, and some students who are functioning at the 10th grade level and have a mental age of 16. These age range differences are based on general ability which is a composite of a number of different kinds of verbal, numerical, and spatial scores. The schools have taken steps to reduce the degree of individual differences found in the classroom. These steps have involved various kinds of ability groupings. The approach that appears to have to have been most successful in reducing the degree of individual differences found in the classroom is grouping students based on their ability levels in specific subject matter areas. However, even this approach has been only minimally satisfactory. The degree of individual differences found in these classes, while reduced from those in classes when grouping was based on general ability, still contains ranges of abilities that span a number of years.

Promoting positive signal learning experiences and avoiding negative signal learning experiences require that we establish educational objectives that are appropriate for the wide range of ability levels that exist in the class. Educational objectives are deemed appropriate if the psychological distance from where the student is at the time instruction begins, to the point to where he or she is to go, is neither too great nor too small. The student should be able to attain the goal in a reasonably short period of time, and without too much frustration. The wide spread in ability levels in any given classroom makes it apparent that what is an appropriate educational objective for one student is an inappropriate objective for another. The problem that arises when we establish the same educational objective for the entire class occurs because if the objective is appropriate for a student whose ability level lies in the middle of the class, the objective is likely to be too difficult for a student in the lower ability level, and may already have been attained by the student with high ability. In this situation, there is no way to avoid exposing many students to negative signal learning experiences.

Rule 2: **Do not leave your affective objectives to be attained in an incidental fashion.**

Specify your affective objectives and plan for their attainment. We must keep our affective objectives in mind so that we can both provide signal learning experiences consistent with the attainment of the objectives, and avoid negative signal learning experiences that are inconsistent with the attainment of the objectives.

Keeping our affective objectives in mind allows us to use them to guide the activities that go on in the classroom. Remember, while we can choose not to provide learning experiences that affect the attainment of our cognitive psychomotor objectives, we cannot choose not to affect the attainment of our affective objectives. Everything that we do is likely to affect the attainment of the affective objectives in one way or another. We must consciously strive to provide positive signal learning experiences in which positive unconditioned stimuli are presented immediately following learning activities, and to avoid negative signal learning experiences by eliminating the negative unconditioned stimuli from the classroom.

Rule 3: Use positive evaluation procedures.

We need to evaluate instructional progress in a manner that will keep learning and learning-related activities from becoming conditioned aversive stimuli.

Most negative signal learning episodes found in the classroom seem to stem from the process of evaluating student progress. These signal learning episodes occur when students fail to do well on tests, projects, or other activities that go on in the classroom. The result is that the indicators of failure (criticism, low grades, and punishment) become paired with classroom objects or events to create negative signal learning episodes like the one shown below:

```
                              Criticism
Specific Classroom            Low Grades
Objects or Events             Punishment         Anxiety
        Sc                         Su --------------R

Specific Classroom
Objects or Events             Anxiety
       Sc_a-------------------- R
```

In the end, the negative signal episodes cause anxiety to become associated with the objects and events in the classroom. This in turn, causes the students to withdraw from them.

Positive evaluation procedures are only possible if we establish educational goals that are appropriate for the students. If this is not done, there is a danger that the psychological distance from where the students are, to where they are to go, will be too great. When this occurs, the students are likely to experience negative rather than positive signal learning experiences.

Positive approaches to evaluation require that we identify and reinforce desired responses; while we at the same time help the students to learn from their errors. We

41

learn from our errors. When we get feedback from authorities or from the environment that our position is wrong, we tend to modify our position in a way that is consistent with that feedback. We have to help students identify their errors. At the same time, however, we cannot reinforce the errors themselves. In using a positive approach to evaluation, we need to try to avoid punishing errors while at the same time reinforce the thinking process through which students make use of their errors to correct their responses.

Rule 4: Avoid punishment.

Every incidence of punishment tends to create a signal learning episode. This is because punishment is an unconditioned stimulus, and all that is needed for signal learning to occur is the presence of an unconditioned stimulus. Anything that the learner is focused on immediately prior to the presentation of the unconditioned stimulus tends to become a conditioned aversive stimulus. In this way the effects of punishment tend to generalize. The effect of the use of punishment in the classroom is to create signal learning episodes which turn teachers, school, learning, and learning-related activities into conditioned aversive stimuli which create anxiety for the learner. These stimuli are then avoided, thus creating a situation that is incompatible with student growth.

Rule 5: Do not allow others in the classroom to turn learning and learning related stimuli into conditioned aversive stimuli.

Classmates, as well as the teacher, can be sources of punishment in the classroom. Classmates punish each other for any number of reasons. This punishment is most serious when it is related to the learning activities that go on in the classroom. Peer criticism of attempts to read, sing, solve mathematics problems, give speeches, etc. are harmful because it tends to cause these activities to become conditioned aversive stimuli which causes anxiety for the learner. The result is that these activities are avoided. We need to do everything we can to see that this peer punishment does not occur.

Rule 6: Recondition students for whom school and school related activities have become conditioned aversive stimuli.

We have many students for whom school activities are already conditioned aversive stimuli at the time they enter the classroom. For these students, reading, mathematics, sports, teachers, etc. cause anxiety. The response of the students is to attempt to escape from the anxiety by avoiding the activities. The problem arises because the avoidance of these activities is likely to limit the growth of the students.

Our task in this situation is to try to break the connection between the activities and the anxiety. This is done through the process of reconditioning the activities. In reconditioning the activities we need to establish conditions in which the activities become paired with positive unconditioned stimuli. If mathematics causes anxiety, we can recondition it by establishing signal learning episodes such as the one shown below.

```
                              Praise              Positive
                              Recognition         Emotional
    1.   Mathematics          Reward              Response
              Sc                         Su -----------------------R


                              Positive
                              Emotional
    2.   Mathematics          Response
              Sc  -------------------R
```

If the signal learning occurs as shown in the diagram, the connection between mathematics and anxiety will be broken, and the student will have no reason to withdraw from it.

The breaking of the connection between the activity and anxiety through the process of reconditioning requires consistency. Once we have begun the process of reconditioning, care must be taken to insure that negative unconditioned stimuli never are allowed to slip back into the signal learning episodes. If these negative unconditioned stimuli are again associated with the activity after the reconditioning process has begun, the reconditioning process will either take much longer or never be completed.

Rule 7: Use stimulus discrimination. Help the students to discriminate that aversive unconditioned stimuli are not present in the classroom.

We encounter many students in our classrooms who are highly anxious, but for whom we are unable to identify any one conditioned aversive stimuli. Without a conditioned aversive stimulus, reconditioning is impossible. When this situation occurs, we must utilize stimulus discrimination. We need to work to help these students discriminate the aversive unconditioned stimuli that originated their anxiety are not present in the classroom. If we can help them make this discrimination, and at the same, create signal learning situations in which classroom activities are associated with positive unconditioned stimuli, we can help to reduce the general anxiety level of the students. This in turn will reduce their tendency to avoid the learning activities that go on in the classroom.

Summary

Signal learning or classical conditioning is the type of learning through which an emotional response becomes attached to a stimulus which previously could not elicit the response.

It is through signal learning that the students acquire their emotional responses to school, teachers, subject matter, tests, and learning activities. Students, who have positive signal learning experience in connection with the above, tend to "like", "enjoy," or "appreciate" them, while students who primarily have negative signal learning experiences associate with these objects and activities come to "hate," "dislike", or "abhor" them.

Signal learning involves three different components: a conditioned stimulus, an unconditioned stimulus, and a response. When the conditioned stimulus is followed closely in time by an unconditioned stimulus which elicits an involuntary, emotional response, the conditions are right for signal learning to occur. Signal learning has occurred when the conditioned stimulus becomes capable of eliciting the same response as the unconditioned stimulus. No new response is learned in signal learning. The result of signal learning is that a stimulus which previously could not elicit an involuntary, emotional response becomes able to elicit one.

The signal learning that goes on in our classrooms needs to be planned and controlled. If it is not, too many signal learning experiences occur that are incompatible with our affective goals. There are three factors that make failure to plan and control signal learning detrimental to our affective instruction. First, the students cannot keep from being conditioned. This is because motivation plays no part in signal learning. Second, all that is necessary for signal learning to occur is the presentation of an unconditioned stimulus. When it is presented, anything that the student is focused on prior to the unconditioned stimulus tends to become a conditioned stimulus. The conditioned stimulus then becomes capable of eliciting the same emotional response as the unconditioned stimulus. Third, a signal learning experience tends to accompany every act of evaluation. The evaluation of student progress normally involves the indicators of success or failure. These indicators over a period of time have come to function as positive and negative unconditioned stimuli. When these indicators follow our learning experiences, the conditions are right for signal learning to occur. Our task is to plan and control the learning environment so that the signal learning experiences our students are exposed to are positive.

Seven rules are presented for controlling the signal learning that occurs in the classroom. These rules are concerned with working toward the individualization of instruction, planning the signal learning experiences, using positive evaluation procedures, avoiding punishment, controlling the signal learning experiences provided by class members, reconditioning the conditioned aversive stimuli that already exist in the classroom and using stimulus discrimination in affective instruction .

44

A number of classroom situations are described below. Read them carefully, and diagram and label the signal learning experiences that are likely to occur. There may be more than one signal learning experience in each situation.

1. Ms. Callahan, the music teacher, feels that each student must earn the right to participate in singing groups, band, and orchestra. She requires each student to compete for openings in the activities. A student may challenge any other student, and attempt to out-sing or out-play him/her. In these playoffs Ms. Callahan is the judge. The losers sit in the class and are not allowed to challenge again until they recite before the class a record of their efforts which they feel will qualify them to make a new challenge.

2. Joe Flynn directs his teaching at the middle ability level students. He does this because he feels that if he directs it to the high ability students it will be too difficult for the rest of the students, and if he directs it to the lower-ability students everyone else would be bored.

3. Mr. Bemish teaches the honors course in American history. He uses a college-level text, and requires extensive reading outside of class. In addition, he requires a well footnoted research paper of high quality. He justifies this by saying that he wants to prepare his students for college. He gives few "A's" and many "C's" and "D's".

4. Mrs. O'Hara took a course from a nearby university in which she learned about using the normal curve in assigning grades. She now uses it in all of her classes. In all of her grading she gives 60% C's, 32% B's and D's and 4% A's and F's. She justified this on the basis that all human characteristics are normally distributed.

5. Jean, the specialized student teacher, has decided to teach her class five important computational skills. She has made a progress chart with room for five check marks. To motivate her students she has announced that the first student to get five checks will get a large candy bar. The next five finishers will get a small candy bar and the rest will get gum.

6. Diagram and label a signal learning experience to which you have been exposed.

References

Bower, G. H., & Helgard, E. R. (1981). _Theories of learning_. Englewood Cliffs, NJ: Prentice-Hall.

Cook, W. (1948). Individual differences and curriculum practices. _Journal of Educational Psychology_, _39_,141-148.

Gagne, R. M. (1985). _The conditions of learning and theory of instruction_. New York: Holt, Rinehart & Winston.

Hovland, C. I. (1937). The generalization of conditioned response. _Journal of General Psychology_, _17_, 125-148.

Kimble, G. A. (1967). _Foundations of conditioning and learning_. New York: Appleton.

Pavlov, I. P. (1927). _Conditioned reflexes_ (G. V. Anrep, Trans.). New York: Oxford.

Ringness, T. A. (1975). _The affective domain in education_. Boston: Little Brown.

Watson, J. B., & Raynor, R. (1920). Conditioned emotional reacting. _Journal of Experimental Psychology_, _3_, 1-14.

CHAPTER 3

OPERANT LEARNING AND OUR AFFECTIVE INSTRUCTION

Behavioral Objectives for Chapter 3

When you have completed the chapter, you should be able to:

1. identify examples of specific affective objectives.

2. differentiate between signal learning and operant responses.

3. recognize the kinds of behaviors teachers teach.

4. differentiate the behaviors, and recognize the current emphasis in growth and classroom management objectives.

5. recognize when teachers are providing operant learning experiences that affect the attainment of their affective objectives.

6. recognize where the teacher's attention should be focused in attempting to change behavior.

7. define and identify new examples of positive reinforcement.

8. define and identify new examples of negative reinforcement.

9. define and identify new examples of extinction.

10. define and identify new examples of punishment.

11. define and identify new examples of shaping behaviors through successive approximation.

12. identify the ways operant learning differs from signal learning

13. define and identify new examples of the reinforcement of an incompatible response.

14. identify the effect that punishment has on both the person who is punished and the person doing the punishing.

15. recognize the relationship of extinction to schedule of reinforcement.

16. recognize the effect of punishment on the punished behavior.

17. define and identify new examples of the use of escape and defense behaviors.

18. recognize the relationship of escape and defense behaviors to negative reinforcement.

19. recognize how psychologists view defense and escape mechanisms.

20. recognize signal learning episodes likely to cause people, places, content or objects to become conditioned aversive stimuli.

21. recognize the relationship of punishment to signal learning.

22. recognize what is involved in the elimination of escape and defense behaviors.

23. recognize the conditions that suggest that a behavior is maintained by negative reinforcement.

24. recognize the procedures available to teachers for reducing escape and defense behaviors.

25. given situations involving the reinforcement of responses that are incompatible with escape and defense behaviors, predict outcomes.

26. recognize the relationship of conditioned aversive stimuli to negative reinforcement.

27. recognize the effect of punishment on escape and defense behaviors.

28. given signal learning and the subsequent escape and defense diagram, interpret and identify the parts.

Discovering the Problem

Form small groups and examine the list of specific affective objectives that you derived after completing Chapter 3. Write down three of the affective objectives, and describe how you would go about trying to attain them. Also describe any learning experiences you might provide that are incompatible with the attainment of the objectives.

The Importance of Operant Learning to Affective Instruction

Operant learning and signal learning combine to affect the attainment of our affective goals. Signal learning affects the attainment of our affective goals by determining the kind of emotional response our students come to associate with school and school-related activities. Operant learning affects the attainment of our affective goals by determining the frequency or duration with which our students perform desired and undesired behaviors.

It is through operant learning that we teach our students to study more, hand in assignments, come to class on time, take part in class discussions, or participate in different kinds of learning activities. It is also through operant learning that we teach our students to shout out in class, avoid studying, come to class late, talk back to us, and avoid new learning experiences. We generally have recognized that we teach our students their desirable behaviors. However, the idea that we teach them their undesired behaviors has not occurred to many of us.

Operant learning is an important type of learning for affective instruction because it is through operant learning that desired and undesired student behaviors become strengthened or weakened. The operant learning experiences to which we expose our students can be either positive or negative. If the operant learning experiences to which they are exposed are positive, the result is the strengthening of desired behaviors and the weakening of undesired behaviors. Conversely, if the operant learning responses are negative, the result is the strengthening of undesired behaviors or the weakening of desired behaviors.

Operant learning is vital for the attainment of our important growth objectives. We generally have not recognized this. We have tended to view operant learning as either a means for classroom control or as a lower form of learning which is only appropriate for achieving memory goals. Operant learning, however, can be used to increase the frequency or duration with which our students perform highly important behaviors related to becoming more independent, more creative, more self-confident, more skillful learners or more adequate problem solvers. It is too important a type of learning to be used in the limited way that it has been used. We need to recognize its potential and use it for promoting the attainment of our important growth objectives.

We need to plan and control the operant learning experiences that go on in our classrooms. They should not be left incidental to the instructional process. This is because operant learning experiences, like signal learning experiences, occur with or without our planning. They are likely to occur when we smile, nod our head, acknowledge a response, provide a privilege, give a reward, or ignore a student response. It also occurs when peers follow a student response with these behaviors. If these experiences are not planned and controlled, too many of them tend to be incompatible with the attainment of our educational goals.

Ignoring operant learning is dangerous. This is because operant learning shares many of the characteristics of signal learning.

First, the operant learning experiences that occur in the classroom affect the attainment of all of our objectives. They directly affect the attainment of our specific affective objectives by determining the frequency or duration with which our students perform the behaviors specified in the objectives. They also affect the attainment of our cognitive or psychomotor objectives by determining how frequently or for what duration our students perform the behaviors necessary for the learning to occur.

Second, operant learning experiences go on whether or not we plan for them to occur. They are provided whenever we or the peer group respond or fail to respond to student behaviors. When we do not systematically plan and control the operant learning experiences that occur in the classroom, too many of the learning experiences end up weakening desired and strengthening undesired student behaviors.

Third, the operant learning experiences to which we expose our students can be either positive or negative. The experiences are positive or negative depending on the behavior that is strengthened. The experiences are positive if they strengthen desired behaviors or weaken undesired behaviors. The experiences are negative if they strengthen an undesired behavior or weaken a desired behavior.

51

The efficient use and control of operant learning in the classroom requires the use of the model of the educational act. We must construct our specific affective objectives, incorporate them into the model, and then use the principles of operant learning to facilitate their attainment. The stating of the specific affective objectives makes the behaviors a focus of our attention. Once this occurs, we are in a position to design learning experiences that will strengthen the desired objectives and weaken the undesired behaviors contained in the negative objectives.

The Nature of Operant Learning

Operant learning is learning under the control of the events which follow a response. The conditions necessary for it to occur have been well established (Skinner, 1953). For example, if a baby pulls at the dress of its mother, and receives a cookie, the conditions are right for operant learning to occur. In this example, operant learning has occurred when the frequency with which the baby pulls at the dress increases.

Operant learning can be diagrammed as follows (Gagne, 1985):

$$Ss \text{ -------- } R, R$$

In the diagram, the capital "S" stands for an external stimulus that is observable. In the situation described above the "S" is the mother or the cookie. The small "s" represents an internal stimulus that is not observable. In the case of the baby it is likely to be hunger. In operant learning, it is helpful, but not necessary, that we know what is acting as the stimulus. In fact, many psychologists refuse to speculate about the stimulus in an operant learning sequence when it cannot be directly observed. They are much more interested in what is maintaining or strengthening a behavior than what is stimulating it.

The arrow which follows the stimulus in the diagram indicates the response that follows is a voluntary, precise response such as the baby pulling at its mother's dress. This response is different from the emotional, involuntary response found in signal learning.

The "R" that follows the arrow in the diagram represents the voluntary response that is affected in operant learning. The response that was strengthened in the mother-baby incident was the voluntary act of pulling at the dress.

The second "R" in the diagram is used to indicate that the response was followed by the presentation of a reinforcer. A reinforcer is anything following a response which increases the probability that the response will be repeated. The reinforcer in the incident of the mother and the baby was the presentation of the cookie.

Operant learning is learning that is under the control of the events which follow the response. There are four different kinds of events that can follow a response which has an effect on its frequency or duration. These are positive reinforcement, negative reinforcement, punishment, and extinction.

52

An easy way to discriminate the differences among the four concepts is through the use of the following diagram. In the diagram each of the processes is defined by the column and row of the cell that it occupies.

	Presenting	Withdrawing	Withholding
Positive Reinforcer	a) Process: Positive Reinforcement	b) Process: Punishment	c) Process: Extinction
Aversive Stimulus	d) Process: Punishment	e) Process: Negative Reinforcement	

The process in cell "a" is "positive reinforcement." As it is defined above, the process of positive reinforcement involves the presentation of a positive reinforcer. Any behavior that is followed by the presentation of a positive reinforcer will be strengthened. For example, if a smile is a positive reinforcer for a student, smiling after the student has made a response to a question would be an example of positive reinforcement.

It is important for us to discriminate that anything that follows an act and increases its frequency or duration is a positive reinforcer. The reverse is also true. Anything that follows an act and does not increase its frequency or duration is not a positive reinforcer. We cannot say that we reinforced the student, and that it did not strengthen the behavior. This is because if the behavior was not strengthened, reinforcement did not occur.

The process of "punishment" is defined by both cell "b" and cell "d" in the diagram. This indicates that there are two different ways of defining punishment. In cell "b" punishment is defined as the withdrawing of a positive reinforcer. This kind of punishment occurs when we take away privileges currently possessed by a student. Note that the privileges are taken away, not withheld. In cell "d" the process of punishment is defined as the presentation of an aversive stimulus. When we physically punish, criticize or ridicule a student, the process is punishment because an aversive stimulus is presented.

The process of "extinction" is defined by cell "c". The process of extinction is defined as the withholding of a positive reinforcer. When we ignore a student who is performing an act in an attempt to gain our attention, we are involved in the process of extinction. Note the difference between withholding a positive reinforcer and withdrawing a positive reinforcer. The withdrawing of a positive reinforcer, i.e., taking candy away, is an example of punishment. The withholding of a positive reinforcer, i.e., not presenting the candy after a response, is an example of extinction.

The extinguishing of a response requires that we be consistent. Once we have started to remove the reinforcement that has been maintaining a behavior, we must make

53

sure the reinforcement does not occur again. If reinforcement is allowed to reoccur once the extinction process has begun, the behavior becomes established on an intermittent reinforcement schedule, and the extinction process becomes more difficult.

"Negative reinforcement" is defined by cell "e". Negative reinforcement occurs when an aversive stimulus is withdrawn. Any behavior that leads to the reduction or withdrawal of an unpleasant stimulus tends to become stronger. For example, if the act of rationalizing a behavior leads to the reduction of anxiety. The act of rationalizing behaviors will tend to be strengthened.

An error that we often make is to confuse negative reinforcement with punishment. They are not the same. The effect of negative reinforcement is to strengthen a behavior. The effect of punishment is to temporarily reduce or suppress a behavior.

Practice Exercise 3-1

Below are the descriptions of a number of events. Examine the events, and see if you can determine the process involved. After each event, write down the process involved (i.e., positive reinforcement, negative reinforcement, extinction, punishment, or none of the above), and attempt to justify your answer.

1. John receives an "A" on a paper.

2. Henry is told that his response is correct.

3. Helen repeats the sound of a hard "a" after being told her response is correct.

4. Marilyn receiving praise for a correct response.

5. Vern doing more division problems after being told his response was correct.

6. Bill being spanked.

7. Joe practices his speech and finds that his practice reduces his anxiety. He now practices for every speech.

8. Carol has her candy taken away.

9. Joan is upset because she feels the mechanic at the garage charged her too much. She goes to see him, the situation is corrected, and she feels better. She is now going to see her teacher whom she feels gave her too low a grade.

10. Albert receives a failing grade on a paper.

11. Florence wants to be in the play. The idea of trying out before others causes her anxiety. She does not try out, and her anxiety goes away. She does not try out for the next play either.

12. Peter is very anxious about mathematics. He starts to daydream in class, and finds that it reduces his anxiety. He now daydreams most of the time.

Using Operant Learning to Attain Our Positive Affective Objectives

Psychologists have discovered a number of principles of operant learning which we can use for facilitating the attainment of our affective goals. Below, these principles have been incorporated into rules that will aid us in strengthening desired and reducing undesired student behaviors.

Rules for Strengthening Desired Behaviors

Positive affective objectives all have one thing in common. They are concerned with strengthening desired student behaviors. In its simplest form our task in attaining our positive affective objectives is to find ways of reinforcing these behaviors. For this reason all of the rules below are concerned with things we can do that will strengthen the desired behaviors specified in our affective objectives.

Rule 1: Help your students to discriminate which behaviors are to be reinforced.

We have two approaches we can use to help our students discriminate the desired behaviors that are to be reinforced.

First, we can wait until the desired behavior occurs, and then reinforce it. This approach works well when the desired behavior occurs frequently enough so that the wait to reinforce the behavior does not become too long. It is often used to strengthen behaviors related to such things as cleanliness and appearance which are sensitive topics which we may not wish to approach directly. In cases like the above we can wait until the student improves some aspect, and then take some action to reinforce the behavior. The act of reinforcing the behavior helps the student discriminate the desired behavior.

Second, we can help our students discriminate which responses are to be reinforced by contracting with the students. Contracting will be discussed in greater detail later. However, in the process of contracting we make an agreement with the students in which we indicate that if they perform the desired behaviors, they can have a specific reward.

Contracting is important particularly when the behavior to be strengthened is a weak behavior that is unlikely to occur on its own. Many of the desired behaviors we would like to strengthen occur so infrequently that we must cause them to occur, and then reinforce them if we are to be successful in strengthening them. The process of contracting to help the students discriminate the behaviors that are to be reinforced is important especially when we have been the source of reinforcement for an incompatible, undesired behavior. The danger occurs when the students discriminate that the undesired behavior is not being reinforced, and cannot discriminate what behavior is to be reinforced. The situation is likely to lead to a feeling of rejection.

For example:

> Mrs. Willard, the teacher of a class of emotionally handicapped children, determined that she was inadvertently reinforcing disruptive behaviors by providing extra attention for those students who disturbed the class. She concluded that she would stop acknowledging the behaviors by giving the student attention. After the process of extinction was begun, a student was heard to complain, "Mrs. Willard does not like me any more."

The situation resulted because Mrs. Willard failed to help the students discriminate which responses would be followed by reinforcement. The students recognized that they were no longer being reinforced, and did not know what to do to gain reinforcement.

A situation similar to the one described above occurred in the case of Bill, an orphan, who had been moved from foster home to foster home.

> Mr. Walters was aware of Bill's situation, and tried to make him feel more secure by giving him extra attention. It soon became apparent, however, that Bill had an insatiable need for attention, and Mr. Walters found himself spending large portions of time on the project of making Bill feel more secure. An analysis of the situation led Mr. Walters to conclude that he was reinforcing Bill for dependent acts. He decided that he would begin to treat Bill like any other student, and stop reinforcing dependent acts. The result of Mr. Walter's actions was that Bill felt rejected.

In the process of trying to extinguish Bill's dependent behavior, Mr. Walters failed to help Bill discriminate in what other ways he could gain reinforcement. Mr. Walters should have established the goal that Bill become more independent, and then helped him discriminate the independent behaviors that were to be reinforced.

Rule 2: When the desired behavior occurs, reinforce it.

Our positive affective objectives all indicate a desire to strengthen the frequency or duration of behaviors necessary for student growth. The process through which we strengthen these behaviors is positive reinforcement. Positive reinforcement occurs when the behavior is followed by the presentation of a positive reinforcer. In its simplest form our task in attaining our positive affective objectives is to find ways of eliciting the desired student behaviors, and then making sure they are followed by a positive reinforcer.

Rule 3: Make sure the reinforcer that follows the desired behavior is reinforcing for the student.

We must make sure that the reinforcer that we use to strengthen the desired student behaviors is reinforcing. One of the most common errors we make in attempting to attain our affective objectives is to think we have reinforced a behavior when we have not. By definition a reinforcer is anything following a response that increases the probability the response will be repeated. Whether the presentation of an object or event is reinforcing or not depends upon the effect it has on the behavior which preceded it. If it has the effect of strengthening the behavior, it is considered to be reinforcing regardless of the way it is perceived by the individual presenting the reinforcement. We often use the term "reward" interchangeably with "reinforcement." While it is sometimes helpful to think of them as having common elements, there are pitfalls in doing so. "Reward" usually implies a judgment as to the relative goodness or desirability of an object or event. The concept of "reinforcement" on the other hand is only concerned with whether or not the behavior was strengthened. We may consider an event such as scolding to be undesirable--it could hardly be called a reward, but if the effect of scolding a child is to strengthen the behavior which preceded it, we must conclude that the scolding was reinforcing for the child. In a similar fashion, teacher praise or recognition is usually considered to be a reward. However, whether the praise or recognition is reinforcing for the student or not depends upon the way that it is perceived by the student. If the praise or recognition does not strengthen the behavior it follows, it cannot be considered a positive reinforcer. In instances in which the rapport between the student and the teacher has deteriorated, teacher praise and recognition could conceivably even become an aversive stimuli.

When we confuse positive reinforcement and reward by thinking in terms of what is pleasing to us, it is difficult to achieve our affective objectives. The confusion of terms is likely to create situations in which we:

1. reinforce undesirable behavior while believing that we are punishing it (i.e., scolding a student, who perceives the scolding as a form of attention).

2. give rewards for desired behaviors but fail to reinforce them (i.e., rewarding a student, who does not like to read, for a creative act by sending him to the library).

Rule 4: When a desired behavior occurs, reinforce it as quickly as possible.

"Contiguity," an important concept in signal learning, is also an important concept in operant learning. In general, the greater the contiguity between the response and the reinforcement, the more rapid the learning. For example, the attainment of specific affective objectives, such as increasing the probability that Vince will listen to directions or that Jane will use her study time to do her homework, will be increased if we add contiguity to the learning experience by presenting the reinforcer immediately after the response.

It should be pointed out, however, that humans, unlike lower animals, are able to relate events, activities, and behaviors mentally to reinforcers which may occur long after these responses have occurred. In addition, they are able to perceive

59

reinforcers in the future for acts and behaviors undergone in the present. Hence, a student may go through many experiences at school which may be nonreinforcing at that time in anticipation of reinforcing events which may occur in the future.

Nevertheless, we should integrate the concept of "contiguity" into instructional planning when working with affective objectives. It helps promote the strengthening of the desired behaviors.

Rule 5: Shape the desired student behavior by reinforcing each successive approximation toward the desired goal.

Most positive affective objectives cannot be attained as the result of any one learning experience. Attaining affective objectives such as:

Eric will hand in neater papers.
Jill will hand in more complete assignments.
Jim will increase the amount of such time spent studying.

requires a gradual shaping of behavior. Getting Eric to hand in neater papers, Jill to hand in complete assignments, or Jim to increase his study time is best attained through the process of reinforcing each successive approximation of the desired goal.

The reinforcement of each successive approximation toward the goal requires that we reinforce the learner for any response that is nearer to the desired behavior than previous responses. For example, if Eric hands in a paper that is neater than those he has handed in before, he should be reinforced. Thereafter, he should be reinforced each time he hands in a paper that is as neat or neater than previous papers. Jill and Jim should be reinforced for each response that is a closer approximation of the desired response than those emitted previously. Jill should be reinforced each time a complete or more complete paper is handed in, and Jim should be reinforced for progressively longer periods of studying. Responses that are not as close an approximation to the desired behavior as those previously made should not be reinforced.

Rule 6: Make sure the initial step toward the goal specified in your positive affective objective is small enough so that you get a chance to reinforce the student.

A second common error that we make in trying to attain our positive affective objectives is to make the initial step required before reinforcement takes place too large. If the initial step is too large, we may never get the opportunity to begin the shaping process. This is because we never get a chance to reinforce the initial step toward the desired goal. If, in the case of the affective objectives mentioned above, Eric never hands in a neat paper, Jill never completes an assignment, and Jim never spends any class time studying, we should begin the shaping process by reinforcing very small steps toward the goal. If Eric hands in a paper in which part of it is neater than what he has done before, we should reinforce him for that portion of the paper. We should then proceed to reinforce each successive approximation toward the goal of neat papers. Attaining the affective objective set for Jill may require that we begin by reinforcing her for partially complete assignments. Similarly, if Jim constantly wanders about the room after being given an assignment, he should be reinforced for working in his seat for even short periods of time.

Rule 7: Use many small reinforcers rather than a few large reinforcers in attempting to attain your specific affective objectives.

Frequency of reinforcement is more important than size of reinforcer in attempting to bring about changes in behavior. Another way of saying this is that the use of one large reinforcer is less effective for achieving behavior change than using a series of small reinforcers. Promising the student a major reinforcer for the attainment of an objective involving a major behavior change is not as effective as presenting a small reinforcer for each step the student takes toward the major goal.

Most of the important affective objectives of the teacher cannot be attained by exposure to any one learning experience. Instead, they require the shaping of the desired behavior by the reinforcement of successive approximations of the desired behavior. Both the teacher presenting the reinforcer and the student being reinforced often fail to recognize the above. The example below is used to illustrate what occurs when two different approaches to attaining the same motivational objective are used.

> Mr. Orwell and Mr. Nolan both have a high ability, low achieving student in their class. They have both determined that the student likes to go fishing. Mr. Orwell tells the student in his class that if he earns an "A" for the term he will take him fishing. Mr. Nolan determines how well the students typically performs in his class, and offers the student points that can be accumulated toward the fishing trip each time his daily performance meets or exceeds the level previously attained.

There is little question that Mr. Nolan will be more successful than Mr. Orwell in attaining the objective. It is likely that both boys entered into the agreement with their teacher with equal enthusiasm. Mr. Orwell has made the mistake of assuming that the way to make a major change in the behavior of the student was to offer him a major reinforcer on an all-or-nothing basis. The agreement that Mr. Nolan made with the student in his class allowed him to reinforce the student for each step along the way to the goal. The use of the points make it possible for him to reinforce the student many times instead of relying on one major reinforcer.

Rule 8: Move from a continuous to an intermittent reinforcement schedule.

61

Our ultimate goal is the development of self-directed, self-motivated students. The affective objectives and the learning experiences we provide should be constructed with this idea in mind. The approach we use depends to a large degree on the operant strength of the desired behavior. When the operant strength of the desired behavior is very low, we must begin by using a schedule in which the student is reinforced for each successive approximation of the desired goal. However, as the operant strength of the desired behavior increases, we should begin to move from a continuous to an intermittent reinforcement schedule. Moving from a continuous to an intermittent reinforcement schedule is essential if we are to create self-directed, self-motivated students. It should be pointed out, however, that the number of responses that we require before we reinforce the student should be gradually increased in order to avoid extinguishing the behavior. If during the process of trying to move from a continuous to an intermittent reinforcement schedule the student stops performing the response or greatly reduces the frequency with which he performs it, we should return to a continuous schedule. It is helpful to think of self-directed, self-motivated students not as individuals who never need reinforcement from others, but instead view them as individuals who are capable of going for extended periods of time without external reinforcement from others.

Moving from a continuous to an intermittent reinforcement schedule makes it easier for us to distribute reinforcement. If all students were on continuous reinforcement schedules, the task of reinforcing them would be impossible. Many of the behaviors that we specify in our positive affective objectives are already established on an intermittent reinforcement schedule. The task is to find ways of increasing their operant strength. We can do this by increasing the reinforcement schedule so that the behaviors are reinforced more frequently.

Another reason we should move to establish the behaviors on an intermittent reinforcement schedule is because behaviors established on an intermittent reinforcement schedule are more resistant to extinction than behaviors that are continuously reinforced. If we establish a desired student behavior on a continuous reinforcement schedule, and then stop reinforcing the behavior, it will soon cease to occur. However, behaviors established on an intermittent reinforcement schedule will continue to be emitted for a considerable period before they are extinguished.

We can sometimes be successful in attaining our affective objectives by starting right off with the use of an intermittent reinforcement schedule. For example:

> Mr. Christianson taught in an urban school. He found that in the school many students were extremely disorganized. They often came to class without their books, paper or pencils. He observed, however, that even though the students were disorganized, they were still concerned with their grades. Mr. Christianson established the positive affective objective that the students increase the frequency with which they brought these materials to class. He attained the objectives through the use of an intermittent reinforcement schedule. He did this by coming into the class on random days, holding up a pencil, a piece of paper or the text and announcing, "Today, if you have this item, it is worth 10 points which will be used in computing your grade." He found that the intermittent reinforcement schedule was a very powerful tool. In a short period of time nearly all students were bringing the materials to class.

Practice Exercise 3-2

Below are a number of episodes involving individuals who are attempting to use positive reinforcement to strengthen desired student behaviors. Read each episode and attempt to determine whether or not the teacher is likely to be successful in attaining the desired goal. Write your conclusion and the reason for it in the space following the episode.

1. Mr. Graham's objective is that Rose study harder for her examinations. Mr. Graham gives an examination for which Rose studies harder than usual. Mr. Graham returns the examination papers two weeks later.

2. Ms. Skinner's objective is that Lettie hand in completed assignments. Lettie has created many discipline problems for Ms. Skinner, and Ms. Skinner has had to discipline her many times. Ms. Skinner decides to attempt to attain her objective by writing positive comments on the papers Lettie does hand in.

3. Mrs. Mellon's objective is that Mark ask better questions. She decides that she will only respond positively to his "good" questions and will ignore his "poor" questions.

4. Mr. Peters tells his son, who is a "C" student, that if he works hard and gets an "A" this semester he will take him to Florida to scuba dive.

5. Ms. Ibsen has a class of low achieving, poorly motivated students. These students seldom do an assignment. Ms. Ibsen's objective is that the students hand in more assignments. She attempts to accomplish her objective by 1) determining that the class would like to put on a play and 2) giving the students points which can be accumulated toward the play each time there is an increase in the number of assignments handed in.

6. Mrs. Licking has a goal that Spencer become more self-motivated. Her approach to attaining her objective is to give Spencer attention for every assignment that he hands in, and then to begin giving him progressively less attention for the assignments.

Reducing Undesired Behaviors Maintained by Positive Reinforcement

The attainment of many of our positive affective objectives requires that we also be successful in attaining our negative objectives. For example, we cannot hope to be successful in attaining such objectives such as:

increasing the amount of class study time spent studying.

increasing the frequency with which the student comes to class on time.

increasing the frequency with which the student hands in completed assignments.

Unless we are also successful in attaining negative objectives concerned with:

decreasing the amount of class study time spent wandering about the room.

decreasing the frequency with which the student is late for class.

decreasing the frequency with which the student fails to hand in completed assignments.

In attempting to attain negative affective objectives, we should focus attention on what is maintaining the undesired behaviors rather than on trying to determine the original cause of the behavior or speculating about the deep underlying cause of the behavior. Undue concern about what may have happened years ago that led to the behavior or attempting to attribute the behavior to deep underlying psychological problems, such as a lack of self-worth or poor ego strength, is nonproductive. It usually is not possible to determine the original cause with any degree of certainty; and even if it is possible to determine the original cause of undesired behavior, it is not clear what should be done about it. Similarly, even if we are able to successfully label the underlying cause of the behavior, the label does not suggest what needs to be done to change the behavior. On the other hand, if we are able to determine the source of reinforcement for the undesired behavior, we are often in a position to manipulate the reinforcement in such a way that the reinforcement does not follow the behavior.

Rules for Reducing or Eliminating the Undesired Behaviors

Our task in attempting to attain negative affective objectives is to (1) find ways of removing the reinforcement from the undesired behaviors, and (2) reinforce positive responses that are incompatible with the negative behaviors. The ways we can accomplish this are suggested by the rules that follow.

Rule 1: Avoid the tendency to punish undesired behaviors.

We should avoid the tendency to punish undesired student behaviors. For many of us, the tendency to punish undesired behavior is almost a reflex. We tend to punish any behavior that is perceived as threatening. We punish because we are trying to do a good job, and it appears as though the students are trying to keep us from doing it. We punish because we perceive certain student behaviors as a threat. In most cases, however, the punishment creates more problems than it solves.

One problem that is created when we come to rely too heavily on the use of punishment for controlling a desired behavior is a reduction in our ability to control behavior through positive reinforcement. Punishment can create signal learning episodes in which we tend to become a conditioned aversive stimulus. When this occurs, we lose the ability to reinforce desired student behaviors through personal attention. Our attention, smiles, praise, etc. are only reinforcing if the students view them as reinforcing. Once we have lost student rapport through the excessive use of punishment, we have a difficult time using many positive approaches. We need to understand the reasons for punishing, and the effect that it has on us and the student, if we are to avoid the tendency to punish.

When someone is punished, it is assumed that it will cause a change in behavior, and the individual will learn not to perform the undesired act. Psychologists, however, seriously question the value of punishment in changing behavior. Experimental evidence indicates that punishment normally does not extinguish the undesired behavior. It only temporarily suppresses it. After the anxiety that results from the punishment subsides, the undesired behavior often returns more strongly than before. There is some research that indicates if the behavior is not too highly motivated, and the individual has an alternative response available, punishment may help cause a change in behavior. However, most psychologists would agree that the side effects of punishment are too serious to recommend it as a primary means for controlling undesired behavior.

The most serious consequence of punishment for the individual, who is punished, occurs because the anxiety that results from the punishment generalizes through signal learning to anything the punished individual associates it. The consequence is that many stimuli that previously caused little emotional reaction come to cause anxiety. When the individual is punished frequently, such large numbers of conditioned aversive stimuli may be developed that the individual remains in a constant state of anxiety. This can result in a situation in which the individual begins to spend such large amounts of time and energy trying to escape from anxiety, that it can be said they are living primarily to reduce or avoid anxiety.

Punishment is bad for the individual who does the punishing. This is because he is immediately reinforced for punishing by the suppression of the undesired behavior. For this reason, the next time he encounters behavior he feels is undesirable, he will be more likely to punish it. The punisher normally does not notice the reoccurrence of the undesired behavior, and is fooled into believing that punishment works. The reinforcement that the punisher receives after punishing can be used to explain its wide use. For most, the tendency to punish is shown in our behavior when we continue to use punishment even in the face of continuing evidence that punishment does not work with particular individuals.

From a learning point of view, punishment is a questionable procedure because (1) it temporarily suppresses, but does not extinguish the undesired behavior; (2) it only indicates to the punished individual what he should not do, and does not let him know what he should do; and (3) it may lead to the development of anxiety and escape behaviors which are inconsistent with the growth of the individual.

Rule 2: Determine what is reinforcing the undesired behavior.

The first task in attempting to reduce undesired behavior is to determine the source of reinforcement. Negative behaviors like positive behaviors have different operant strength. However, if the behaviors are occurring with any frequency, it is because they are being reinforced. We have to find the source of reinforcement for the behaviors before they can be extinguished.

There are two main sources of positive reinforcement for the undesired behaviors that occur in the classroom--the teacher and the peer group.

We are often the source of reinforcement for the undesired behavior that occur in the classroom. We frequently end up reinforcing undesired behaviors. This occurs because we fail to recognize that whether our responses to student behaviors are reinforcing or not depends on the perception of the students--not on our perceptions. It is possible for us to think that we are punishing a response when we are actually reinforcing it.

A primary example of this is the "Trap of Leaving Well Enough Alone." We fall into the "Trap of Leaving Well Enough Alone" when we fail to reinforce desired behavior, and end up reinforcing undesired behavior. We are most likely to fall into the trap with students who have a high need for attention. We unwittingly fall into the trap when we fail to give the students attention when they perform desired tasks, but give them attention for undesired behaviors.

An example of "Trap of Leaving Well Enough Alone" is shown below:

> The students in Mrs. Kelley's class began the year responding to questions by raising their hand and waiting to be acknowledged. However, by the end of the first term, they were responding to questions by rising out of their seats, frantically waving their hands and shouting, "I know, I know".

The behavior of rising out of the seat, waving their hands, and shouting is occurring because it has been reinforced. At the beginning of the school year, Mrs. Kelley made the mistake of calling on those students who expended the most effort in attempting to be called upon. The students soon discriminated that they were more likely to be called upon if they rose in their seats, waved their hands, and shouted. The undesired behavior was shaped as Mrs. Kelley began calling on a student each time he was noisier than before. At the same time she was reinforcing successively more vigorous hand waving, she was extinguishing the desired responses of raising the hand quietly and waiting to be acknowledged. Sitting quietly and raising the hand was not reinforced because the student was not called upon. Mrs. Kelley fell into the "Trap of Leaving Well Enough Alone," and in the process taught her students to respond to questions by rising in their seats, waving their hands, and shouting. In this case,

Mrs. Kelley should have been more careful to reinforce the students who raised their hands quietly and waited to be acknowledged. This was the "well enough" that she extinguished by "leaving it alone" (i.e., by not reinforcing it).

The undesired behaviors contained in the negative affective objectives are often maintained or strengthened because they are reinforced by peers. The peer group becomes an increasingly important reinforcing agent as the students enter preadolescence, and continues to influence behavior throughout the high school years. The class clown provides the most familiar example of peer reinforcement of undesired behavior. Clowning antics nearly are always reinforced by the laughter and attention received from peers. The kind of attention received by the clowning individual is reinforcing. This is true even though it may not appear to be reinforcing to us. The important point, however, is not how we view the laughter and teasing, but how they are viewed by the student. If the laughter and teasing strengthen the behavior they must be viewed as reinforcing. As most of us are aware, the operant level of clowning behavior can become exceedingly high. The reduction or extinction of the behaviors depends on the identification and removal of the source of reinforcement.

Disruptive behaviors are sometimes reinforced by both us and the peer group. This situation is likely to occur when we have little or no rapport with the students, and becomes visibly upset over the antics of the class. Getting us upset can be reinforcing for some students. This, coupled with the attention they receive from their classmates, creates a situation in which we are likely to lose control of the class.

Rule 3: Take steps to remove the reinforcement that follows the undesired behavior. Be consistent!

Removing the reinforcement that follows the behaviors tends to cause the behavior to be extinguished. Behaviors that are maintained because they have reinforced everytime they occur are easier to extinguish than behaviors that have been established on an intermittent reinforcement schedule. For this reason, it is very important to be consistent when attempting to extinguish the undesired behaviors contained in negative affective objectives. Failure to be consistent can have the effect of changing the reinforcement schedule of the behavior from continuous to intermittent. The establishment of the undesired behavior on an intermittent schedule makes the attainment of the negative objectives more difficult. For example, extinguishing the "shouting out" behavior of Henry by ignoring it will be much more difficult if we break down and occasionally respond to it. This establishes the behavior on an intermittent reinforcement schedule, and make extinction more difficult.

Negative behaviors that are maintained because they have been reinforced by us are the easiest for us to extinguish. This is because we have direct control of the reinforcement. All that is required is that we be consistent in never reinforcing the behavior. Being consistent, however, is not as easy as it sounds. Sometimes we feel good, and sometimes we feel bad. It is when we feel good that we are most likely to reinforce negative behaviors we have previously decided to extinguish. Nevertheless, it is easier for us to remove the reinforcement if we are the source of the reinforcement.

The extinction of negative behaviors that are maintained by peer group reinforcement poses a more complex problem for us than the extinction of behaviors that are maintained as a result of our reinforcement. This is because we do not have direct control over the reinforcement. Extinguishing behaviors that are maintained by peer reinforcement requires that we arrange conditions so that the peer group no longer reinforces the behavior. This will be discussed in greater detail in the Chapter 6.

Stimulus change is a method we can use to remove the reinforcement from an undesired act. Stimulus change is an effective method when we are relatively certain of what is stimulating the behavior. For example, we may be able to determine that Clair is only disruptive when she is sitting near Carol. If such is the case, we can often reduce the undesired behavior by changing the seating arrangement. In this situation it is likely that Clair has come to discriminate that in the presence of Carol disruptive behavior will be reinforced. In a similar fashion, she has discriminated that in the presence of other students, this behavior is not reinforced.

Rule 4: Reinforce responses that are incompatible with the undesired behavior contained in the negative affective objectives.

The reinforcement of incompatible responses occurs when we reinforce a behavior that cannot occur at the same time as the undesired behavior. Van cannot sit quietly in his seat and study, and at the same time wander about the room. If his teacher reinforces him for studying in his seat, he is reinforcing a response that is incompatible with wandering about the room. As "studying" behavior is strengthened, "wandering" behavior is automatically reduced.

If both positive and negative affective objectives have been spelled out, the reinforcement of responses that are incompatible with the undesired behaviors should become almost automatic. This is because in the process of listing the positive and negative objectives the specification of incompatible behaviors to be strengthened occurs naturally. For most negative affective behaviors, there is a positive affective objective which is concerned with strengthening a behavior that is incompatible with the undesired behavior.

Below is the case study of Carla. As a group or in small groups read the case study and attempt to answer the questions that follow.

Case Study

At this point I do not know a great deal about Carla's background. She has lived (at least since she started school) in a small rural town. Both parents are employed at a factory in the town. Carla is the youngest of five children. I have no information concerning her siblings.

Carla is the biggest child in the fifth grade class and with only a couple of exceptions, the largest in the school (which runs grades 5-7). She is 5'4" tall and weighs 177 pounds. She is not a pretty girl. Her hair is short and curly and often greasy and dirty in appearance. Protruding brow ridges and extremely thick glasses are the characteristics one notices quickly. She isn't particularly neat or clean in her personal habits. She gets herself off to school and arrives, at times, in torn t-shirts and shorts. Carla is one of the first in her class to have a good case of teen-age acne.

Academically Carla does pretty well. Her Stanford Achievement Test Average Score (grades 2 and 3) shows her one and one half to nearly two grade levels above her grade in school. In grade 3 she had an average score of 4.82. In grade 4 she had an average score of 4.82, indicating a year Carla did not grow. Currently, in our ability grouped fifth grade, she is in the high ability reading group and low ability math (an unusual combination). I do not teach either of these classes so have no observations here. In Language Arts and Social Studies her work is sloppily and carelessly done. Many things are turned in half finished. Where she should be achieving quite well her work is average or below average.

Carla's relationship with peers is often a shaky deal. Her name is often used to express a comment on her weight. The "very popular" girls uniformly ignore her. She just doesn't exist. Some of the girls not in the group vie for her attention. Carla initiates quite a bit of physical contact with her classmates, both boys and girls. By punching, teasing, knocking others' books on the floor, Carla usually succeeds in finding someone to chase, punch, or tease her.

Carla pokes a lot fun at herself. She is constantly talking about how fat she is. She calls attention to other, thinner people's figures and then compares herself with them. She says she likes me because I am so skinny and pretty--not fat and ugly like she is.

This brings us to her relationship with her teachers. Carla never just raises her hand. She has one knee on the desk and is moaning "ooh-ooh" until she is picked to do something. She calls attention to herself whenever possible. She like to be first in line, and in the front of the room, that is until she discovered I was in the back of the room and then she moved back there. She is always making things for me and giving me things. She sent me a postcard while she was on vacation right after school started.

Her physical mannerisms are nervous and seem involuntary. She is excitable and wrings her hands when corrected. Carla seldom looks you in the eye when talking to you. Her eyes are cast down, often looking at her wringing hands. She follows me around the room often bumping into me or furniture in the room. Her movements are grossly exaggerated and clumsy in execution.

1. List the affective goals you would establish.

2. Justify the goals you established, by explaining why the goals need to be attained.

3. Reduce the affective goals that you have established to specific affective objectives by asking the questions suggested in Chapter 3. List the resulting objectives. Do they meet the six criteria for specific affective objectives?

4. List the negative affective objectives that you would establish.

5. After each negative objective that you have listed, write the probable source of reinforcement for the undesired behavior contained in the objectives.

6. For each negative objective you have stated, construct a positive objective containing a behavior that is incompatible with the behavior contained in the negative objective.

7. Examine the objectives you have constructed, and list the objectives you would focus on attaining initially. Why did you select these?

8. Explain how you would go about extinguishing the undesired behaviors listed in your negative objectives. What would you have to be careful not to do?

9. After reading the case study, suggest positive reinforcers that are likely to be effective in strengthening the student's behavior. Tell why you think they would strengthen the behaviors.

10. Describe how you would go about attempting to strengthen the behaviors specified in your positive objectives. How would you help the student discriminate the behaviors to be strengthened? How would you use successive approximation?

11. How might you use intermittent reinforcement? What would it do for   you?

12. Are there instances where the teacher might have fallen into the "trap of leaving well enough alone?" Where? How did it happen?

13. To what extent has the teacher taught the undesired behaviors?

14. How would you know if the reinforcers you used were reinforcing?

15. How would you insure that you had contiguity between the student responses and the reinforcement?

Reducing Undesired Behaviors Maintained by Negative Reinforcement

The attainment of many of the most important goals and objectives of the school depend on our ability to avoid, reduce or eliminate escape or withdrawal behaviors. We cannot hope to achieve educational goals concerned with developing self-directed, self-motivated students if the students are primarily concerned with escaping or withdrawing from our learning experiences. More specifically, we cannot hope to get our students to increase their reading, mathematics study time, class participation or participation in physical activities if they are actively involved in avoiding reading, mathematics, class participation, and sports. As long as the latter behaviors continue to be maintained or strengthened, we are not going to be successful in strengthening the desired behaviors.

When viewed from the point of view of the schools, escape and withdrawal behaviors are almost always undesirable. The behaviors are behaviors that typically involve avoiding new learning experiences, a condition that is incompatible with student growth.

How We Teach Our Students to Withdraw from Learning Activities

We teach our students to withdraw or escape from the learning activities that go on in the schools. We do not do this intentionally. It occurs more as the result of established school procedures than from any intent on our part. Nevertheless, we are the instruments initiating the learning experiences that tend to cause our students to withdraw from learning activities. We need to understand the process through which this occurs if we are to 1) avoid creating the behaviors and 2) reduce them once they are present.

The process through which we teach our students to withdraw from learning experiences is a two step process.

The first step in teaching the withdrawal behaviors is the establishment of signal learning episodes. Signal learning has remained largely incidental to the instructional process. We have not generally planned and controlled the signal learning that occurs in our classrooms. This has created a condition in which too many negative signal learning experiences occur. These experiences have tended to turn school, school-related activities, and even ourselves into conditioned aversive stimuli that cause the students anxiety. The chief reason this occurs is because all that is really necessary for signal learning to occur is the presentation of an unconditioned stimulus. When this occurs, anything that the students are focused on immediately prior to the presentation of the unconditioned stimulus tends to become a conditioned aversive stimulus that causes the students anxiety. The motivation of the students plays no part in the learning. The students cannot keep from being conditioned. Criticism, low grades, and punishment are the three most common unconditioned stimuli found in the schools. Strictly speaking, low grades and criticism are not unconditioned stimuli. They are, instead, conditioned stimuli that have been paired with unconditioned stimuli for so long that they now function as unconditioned stimuli. Unfortunately, these unconditioned stimuli tend to accompany our evaluation process. We present our students with a learning experience, and then

72

follow it with an evaluation. Too often, and for too many students, the evaluation consists of the presentation of the unconditioned stimuli of criticism, low grades, and punishment. As a result, our learning experiences tend to become conditioned aversive stimuli that cause anxiety.

The second step in teaching the escape or withdrawal behaviors occurs when the students take steps to reduce or eliminate their anxiety. After the signal learning has gone to completion, and the learning activity comes to cause anxiety, the students must take some action to reduce their anxiety. They cannot just hold the anxiety. Any behavior that they perform that tends to reduce or eliminate the anxiety tends to be strengthened by negative reinforcement. The negative reinforcement occurs when any behavior they perform leads to the reduction or elimination of an aversive stimulus. The aversive stimulus in the case of our students is the anxiety, and the behaviors that are strengthened tend to be behaviors that involve withdrawing or escaping from the learning-related objects and activities.

Reading is used in the diagram below to illustrate how students learn to withdraw from a desired behavior. Similar diagrams can be used to illustrate how they learn to withdraw from any activity.

1. Reading

Sc

Criticism
Low Grades
Punishment

Su -------------------- R

Anxiety

2. Reading

Sc_A ----------------------- R

Anxiety

3. (Reading-Anxiety)

Sc_A ----------------------- R

Withdrawal
Crying
Tantrums

Negative Reinforcement
(The withdrawal of the
aversive-stimulus anxiety)

$-R$

The first two lines in the diagram illustrate the signal learning experience. In signal learning experience, the attempts of the student at reading are followed by criticism, low grades, and punishment. The criticism, low grades, and punishment are the unconditioned stimuli in signal learning episodes. If the pairing of reading with criticism, low grades, and punishment is traumatic enough, or if it occurs frequently enough, the signal learning will go to completion as shown in the second line of the diagram. Reading will then come to cause anxiety even in the absence of the unconditioned stimuli.

The third line of the diagram illustrates how the withdrawal behaviors are established and strengthened. After the signal learning has been completed, reading causes anxiety. Whenever the students are confronted with a reading task, they become anxious, and must do something to try to reduce or eliminate the anxiety. They may try a number of behaviors to reduce their anxiety, and any behavior that is successful will be strengthened through the process of negative reinforcement. In the case of our diagram the responses the students made in attempting to reduce their anxiety was to cry, throw tantrums, and withdraw. These behaviors were strengthened because they led to the reduction of anxiety.

How We Can Reduce or Eliminate Withdrawal Behavior

A withdrawal or escape behavior is a behavior that is maintained by negative reinforcement, not positive reinforcement. If a behavior is maintained by positive reinforcement, it is not an escape behavior. We often have questions regarding whether a particular behavior is maintained by positive or negative reinforcement. The same behavior can be maintained by either positive or negative reinforcement. The question of whether the behavior is maintained by positive or negative reinforcement is academic until we try to reduce or eliminate it. Then obvious differences appear. Behaviors maintained by negative reinforcement are more difficult to reduce or eliminate. The reduction of drinking behavior poses different problems depending upon whether the individuals are positively or negatively reinforced for drinking. If the individuals drink because they like the taste of liquor, they are positively reinforced for drinking. However, if they drink because it reduces their fears and anxieties, the drinking is maintained by negative reinforcement and is an escape behavior. The drinking behavior will be considerably more difficult to eliminate in the latter case.

The same situation exists in academically related behaviors. If the students are wandering about the room after being given an assignment because they want the attention of their peers, the wandering behavior is maintained by positive reinforcement. However, if the students are wandering about the room because it reduces the anxiety associated with the school work, the wandering behavior is maintained by negative reinforcement. We can recognize negatively reinforced behavior by the behavior patterns that emerge when we attempt to extinguish the behavior. When we attempt to reduce or eliminate the negatively reinforced behaviors of our students, we are likely to encounter situations in which:

1. the student produces a flurry of escape behaviors that approach panic when forced to take part in the activity.

2. the attempts of the student to stop performing the behavior fail during periods of stress.

3. the student substitutes other withdrawal or defense behaviors when the initial behavior is blocked by the reinforcement of an incompatible response.

The reduction or elimination of withdrawal behaviors is more difficult than the reduction or elimination of behaviors maintained by positive reinforcment. This is primarily because we cannot control the reinforcement. We usually are successful in reducing or eliminating behaviors that are maintained by positive reinforcement. This is because we are often in a position to remove the positive reinforcement. However, we are not normally in a position to remove the negative reinforcement that is maintaining a withdrawal or defense behavior. In the reading episode mentioned previously, for example, there is no way that the teacher can keep the act of withdrawing from reading from reducing anxiety. If we could remove negative reinforcement in the same way as positive reinforcement, we would probably be just as effective in reducing negatively reinforced behavior as we are in reducing positively reinforced behavior.

When attempting to reduce withdrawal or escape behaviors, we should not view the students as escaping from the learning activity, but should instead view them as escaping from the anxiety associated with the activity. This is more than a matter of semantics. The importance of the discrimination becomes apparent when we attempt to change the behavior. If we view the students as escaping from reading, we would perhaps feel justified in forcing them to read. However, if we view them as escaping from the anxiety associated with reading, we readily recognize that forcing them to read may well increase anxiety and promote more escape behavior.

The reduction of withdrawal or escape behaviors requires the reconditioning of the conditioned aversive stimulus. In the case of the reading episode, it would require the reconditioning of reading. If we could recondition reading so that the connection between reading and anxiety was broken, the third line of the diagram would drop out. This is because reading would no longer cause anxiety, and the reason for withdrawing would disappear. The reconditioning of reading requires that reading be paired in signal learning episodes with positive unconditioned stimuli as shown below.

1. Reading	Praise Recognition Reward	Positive Emotional Response
Sc	Su ----------------------	R

2. Reading Positive Emotional Response

Sc -------------------------- R

3. This line in the diagram drops out.

The reconditioning process requires consistency. Once we have started reconditioning, we must make sure that the negative unconditioned stimuli-criticism, low grades, and punishment--are not allowed to again be associated with reading. If the association is allowed to occur again, the reconditioning process will be more difficult.

Read the case study of Harry found below. After you have read the case study, answer the true-false questions that follows. Check your answers against the answers found at the end of the exercise. When this has been done, form groups of 3 or 4, and attempt to tell why the answers are true or false.

The Case Study of Harry

Harry is in my eighth grade physical science class. Harry comes from a very high middle class social-economic background. He often states that he can do whatever he pleases, and that teachers cannot make him do anything he does not want to do. His outward physical appearance is that of a well-adjusted boy. Harry has a "physiological condition" which at times causes him to be very hyperactive during class. He tends to "fool around" and play games with his friends during class. Harry is more immature than the rest of the class. I have often had to separate Harry from his friends because of his "fooling around." He consistently gets out of his assigned seat, and goes to sit with his friends. At times, I have scolded him and given him a detention, but it seems to have no effect on his behavior. In class, he tends to be inconsiderate, impolite, boisterous and mischievous.

Harry is a very slow achiever. He has had relatively few success experiences in school. He is reading at the fifth grade level. His attention span seems to be very short. He does not seem to be able to stay on-task, and tends to talk or "fool around" with his friends while the current topic is being discussed. He puts forth no effort in class, hands in no work, and fails all tests. He does not participate in class, and tends to yell joking remarks to get attention. The class usually laughs at his remarks.

The students in the class tend to recognize and stigmatize Harry as a "dumb student." His peer group perceive Harry as a "big clown." He continually plays the role of "dumb clown" in order to get peer approval.

At times, during laboratory work, Harry does display some interest in those experiments that astonish him. However, the interest usually only lasts for a short period of time. He tends to leave his group to bother other students. Students have complained about Harry being a disturbance and a nuisance.

I have talked to Harry about his beahvior, but it has not caused him to alter his behavior. In addition, I have written comments to his parents about his behavior in class.

1. Giving Harry detention was the most serious form of punishment involved in the case study.

    T   F

2. Peer ridicule was the most serious form of punishment involved in the case study.

    T   F

3. The unconditioned stimulus which most likely initiated Harry's problem was "failure."

   T   F

4. The escape behavior most apparent in Harry's case is rebellion.

   T   F

5. It is probably best to describe Harry as escaping from school work.

   T   F

6. Harry's signal learning response was rebellion.

   T   F

7. Harry's escape behavioar was strengthened primarily because it was reinforced by peers.

   T   F

8. The most obvious unmet "need" in Harry's case was his need for achievement.

   T   F

9. School work is an unconditioned stimulus that creates anxiety for Harry.

   T   F

10. Teacher approval is likely to be the best positive reinforcer for Harry.

    T   F

11. Reading is probably a conditioned aversive stimulus for Harry.

    T   F

12. Harry's hyperactivity is probably inherited.

    T   F

13. Harry's hyperactivity has been established primarily as a result of its positive reinforcement by peers.

    T   F

14. School work can best be described as a conditioned aversive stimulus for Harry.

    T   F

15. Harry's need for peer approval is being adequately satisfied.

    T   F

16. Harry's escape behavior could be extinguished if peer reinforcement were withheld.

    T   F

17. Teachers are conditioned aversive stimuli, and must remain so in Harry's case.

    T   F

18. The reinforcers which are most likely to be effective with Harry in the order of their probable effectiveness would be

    a. teacher praise.
    b. peer group recognition.
    c. academic success.

    T   F

19. The goals that the teacher should strive for in order of importance for Harry are

    a. peer acceptance.
    b. the ability to apply himself to his school work.
    c. acceptance of authority figures.

    T   F

20. A primary task of the teacher is to find a series of academically attainable goals for Harry.

    T   F

Answers: 1-F, 2-F, 3-F, 4-F, 5-F, 6-F, 7-F, 8-F, 9-F, 10-F, 11-T, 12-F, 13-F, 14-T, 15-F, 16-F, 17-F, 18-F, 19-T, 20-T

Rules for Reducing Withdrawal and Escape Behaviors

Rule 1: Do not use punishment either to get students to perform a desired behavior that causes anxiety or to reduce withdrawal or escape behaviors.

The problem that we face in attempting to attain our positive objectives is more difficult if the students are actively withdrawing from the learning activities. For example, if speeches, competitive games, or reading are conditioned aversive stimuli, punishing students to make them perform the behaviors will only act to increase their anxiety and cause further avoidance behavior. The punishment creates additional signal learning episodes which tend to make the activities even more aversive for the students. The punishment of withdrawal behavior has the effect of blocking the behaviors. This increases student anxiety, and creates a condition in which they have no way to reduce their anxiety. The result is increased anxiety, and the greater use of withdrawal behaviors.

Rule 2: Attempt to identify the conditioned aversive stimuli that are causing the anxiety.

Our task in trying to attain affective objectives involving withdrawal behaviors varies depending upon whether or not we are able to identify the conditioned aversive stimulus. If we are able to identify that reading, competitive sports, speech, mathematics, class participation, etc. are conditioned aversive stimuli for the student, we are in a position to begin reconditioning these activities.

Many times, however, neither we nor our students are able to identify the conditioned aversive stimuli that cause the anxiety. This is particularly true if the students have come from highly punitive backgrounds. The excessive use of punishment is likely to have caused all kinds of formerly neutral stimuli to become conditioned aversive stimuli. In situations such as this, the students appear to have a high general level of anxiety which does not seem to be attributable to any particular aversive stimulus. Our inability to identify the conditioned aversive stimulus makes reconditioning impossible. We can, however, attempt to use the process of stimulus discrimination as a basis for reducing the withdrawal behaviors. We can attempt to get the students to discriminate that in our class the conditioned aversive stimuli are not followed by the presentation of an aversive unconditioned stimulus. An example of this process is shown below.

> Miss Fitch has identified Bruce as a highly anxious student. She has not, however, been able to determine the classroom-related activities that lead to the anxiety. Because of the above, she inferred that Bruce's anxiety must be attributed to experiences he has had outside the classroom. If Miss Fitch is careful to use a consistent positive approach with Bruce, she can expect him to begin to discriminate in her class the

conditioned aversive stimuli are not followed by the presentation of aversive unconditioned stimuli. When this occurs, the anxiety will be reduced, and the need to use withdrawal and escape behaviors in the class will be reduced.

Rule 3: **Attempt to recondition the conditioned aversive stimuli that are causing the anxiety.**

The attainment of negative affective objectives involving the reduction of withdrawal behavior requires that we identify the conditioned aversive stimuli that are causing the anxiety. The identification of the conditioned aversive stimuli makes possible the designing of learning experiences to lead to the reconditioning of these stimuli. If the conditioned aversive stimuli can be reconditioned or removed so that they no longer cause the anxiety, the student will no longer need withdrawal behaviors.

The example below illustrates how reconditioning can be achieved.

Jill has never done well in mathematics. Her teacher has noticed that (1) Jill avoids doing her mathematics whenever possible; (2) Jill resorts to copying her friends' papers when pressure is placed upon her to do an assignment; and (3) Jill becomes upset, says that she cannot do the problems, and appears not to try when the teacher attempts to work with her.

The teacher has established the following positive and negative affective objectives for Jill:

Jill will increase the frequency with which she takes part in class discussions.

Jill will increase the frequency with which she completes her own mathematics assignments.

Jill will stop copying her mathematics assignments from others.

Jill will stop becoming upset, and saying that she cannot do the work, when given individual instruction.

The attainment of the objectives requires that the teacher recondition the mathematics by creating signal learning experiences in which mathematics is consistently paired up with positive unconditioned stimuli. This in turn requires that Jill be given work that she is capable of doing. If she is given work that was appropriate for her, the teacher will be able to recondition mathematics as shown below.

		Success Experiences Praise	Positive Emotional
1.	Mathematics	Good Grades	Response

Sc   Su -------------------------- R

2. Mathematics   Positive Emotional Response

Sc ----------------------------------- R

In signal learning, reconditioning by pairing the conditioned aversive stimulus with positive unconditioned stimuli is a more effective way of breaking the conditioned aversive stimuli--anxiety connection--than is extinction alone. Extinction in signal learning occurs when the conditioned stimulus is continually presented without being followed by the unconditioned stimuli (i.e., mathematics without low grades, criticism, etc.). "Consistency" is important in both reconditioning and extinction. Once the process of extinction or reconditioning is begun, care must be taken to make sure that aversive unconditioned stimuli, the criticism, low grades, and punishment, are not allowed to follow the conditioned stimuli. When aversive stimuli are occasionally allowed to follow the conditioned stimulus, the reconditioning process becomes more difficult.

If the reconditioning of mathematics above is successful, mathematics will no longer elicit anxiety, and the withdrawal behaviors will no longer be needed. The withdrawal and defense behaviors will stop because they are no longer needed to reduce anxiety.

Rule 4: Reinforce responses that are incompatible with the withdrawal behaviors.

The behaviors specified in many of our positive affective objectives are incompatible with the withdrawal behaviors of the students. The best results in attaining the positive objectives occur if we create learning experiences which both reduce the withdrawal behaviors and strengthen the desired behaviors. In the example below the behavior contained in the positive objective is incompatible with the withdrawal behavior contained in the negative objective.

Positive objective: The students will increase the duration of available study time spent studying.

Negative objective: The students will decrease the duration of study time spent daydreaming.

The behaviors are incompatible because the students cannot study and daydream at the same time. Strengthening the studying behavior requires reducing daydreaming.

The reinforcement of positive behaviors that are incompatible with the withdrawal behaviors, without reducing the student anxiety, is likely to result in the occurrence of new withdrawal behaviors. An example of the manner in which this occurs is shown below:

>Karen is twelve years old, and is still sucking her thumb. her teacher has established a negative affective objective that Karen stop sucking her thumb. To accomplish this she decided to teach a unit on self-improvement. Each child was asked to select a way in which he/she wanted to improve. Fortunately, Karen's goal was to stop sucking her thumb. To help Karen accomplish her goal, her teacher allowed her to chew gum during class. In addition, because gum chewing was normally not allowed, she established an agreement with the rest of the c ass. The class agreed to allow Karen to chew gum during the week, if they could all chew gum for one period on Friday. This agreement resulted in Karen receiving peer support in her efforts to stop sucking her thumb.

>After the agreement had been in effect for the week, Karen developed a nervous "tick" in which her head would suddenly jerk to the right. The "tick" had been substituted for thumb sucking as a means for reducing anxiety. Reinforcing Karen for chewing gum, a behavior that is incompatible with thumb sucking, blocked her primary method of reducing her anxiety. The anxiety, however, was still present, and because it was still present, Karen had to find some way to reduce it. The "tick" was her answer.

The substitution of one withdrawal behavior for another is a rather common event. It is likely to occur when the teacher reinforces a behavior that is incompatible with a withdrawal behavior, without at the same time taking steps to reduce the anxiety of the student. The substitution of one withdrawal behavior for another can be frightening. This is true especially if the substituted behavior is more undesirable than the behavior being reduced. In the case cited above, the tick stopped a short while later. This probably occurred because the additional attention Karen received from her peers and the teacher led to a reduction of anxiety.

Summary

Operant learning is the type of learning that is used to strengthen or weaken the behaviors specified in our positive and negative affective objectives. It is through the use of the principles of operant learning that we strengthen desired behaviors which are important for the continued growth of our students and weaken undesired behaviors which inhibit their growth.

The operant learning experiences that occur in our classrooms must be planned and controlled. If the operant learning experiences that occur in the classroom are left to occur in an incidental fashion too many learning experiences occur that are inconsistent with our educational goals. This is because the operant learning experiences in the classroom go on with or without our planning, and affect the attainment of all of our objectives. The operant learning experiences that are provided by us and our students can be either beneficial or harmful. Our task is to plan and control these learning experiences so that they lead as directly as possible to the attainment of our affective goals.

Operant learning is learning under the control of the events which follow a response. There are four events which can follow a response and affect the frequency or duration with which the response occurs. These are: 1) the presentation of a positive reinforcer, positive reinforcement, which strengthens the response, 2) the withdrawal of an aversive stimulus, negative reinforcement, which strengthens the response, 3) the withholding of a positive reinforcer, extinction, which weakens the response, and 4) the presentation of an aversive stimulus or the withdrawing of a positive reinforcer, punishment, which temporarily suppresses the response.

The attainment of our educational goals depends upon our ability to use and control the four processes in a manner that promotes student growth.

The strengthening of desired student behaviors is accomplished through the use of the principles of operant learning. These principles can be used as the basis for forming rules that we can use for strengthening desired student behaviors. The rules that we should follow in attempting to strengthen desired student behavior are concerned with:

1. increasing student discrimination of the behavior to be reinforced.

2. using reinforcers that are reinforcing.

3. reinforcing immediately after the response.

4. reinforcing successive approximations toward a goal.

5. making sure the initial step toward the desired goal is small enough so that the student takes it.

6. using many small reinforcers instead of one large reinforcer in attemtping to change behavior.

7. moving from a continuous to an intermittent reinforcement schedule.

The attainment of our affective objective often requires a dual process in which we simultaneously strengthen desired behaviors and weaken undesired behaviors. The dual process is necessary because the positive and negati e behaviors are incompatible. The behaviors are incompatible to the extent that strengthening the desired behavior requires a corresponding reduction in the undesired behaviors.

Many of the undesired behaviors that must be reduced before we can successfully strengthen desired behaviors are maintained through positive reinforcement. There are a number of principles of operant learning that pertain to reducing these behaviors. These principles can be incorporated into rules which can help us reduce these behaviors. The rules are concerned with:

> avoiding the tendency to punish the behaviors.
> determining what is reinforcing the behaviors.
> removing the reinforcement in a consistent manner.
> reinforcing incompatible behaviors.

The attainment of our affective goals often requires that we reduce student withdrawal behaviors. These behaviors are maintained by negative reinforcement. Students utilize these behaviors because they lead to the reduction of withdrawal of their fears and anxieties. The withdrawal behaviors are of concern to us because they are incompatible with student growth. Students cannot continually withdraw from learning activities and grow intellectually and emotionally.

Student withdrawal behaviors are difficult to reduce or eliminate because we are not able to withdraw the negative reinforcement. For example, we cannot keep withdrawing from learning activities from reducing anxiety. The behaviors get stronger because they work--they reduce anxiety. Students generally do not know how to change these behaviors. Without intervention, the behaviors tend to become stronger, and eventually impair growth.

The reduction of withdrawal behaviors requires that we (1) avoid punishment as a means of getting students to reduce withdrawal behaviors, (2) identify the conditioned aversive stimuli that cause the anxiety, (3) recondition the conditioned stimuli that cause the anxiety and (4) positively reinforce desired behaviors that are incompatible with the withdrawal behaviors.

Practice Exercise 3-5

Each episode below involves withdrawal behaviors. Analyze the episodes. Then label the diagrams following each episode so they explain (1) the signal learning episodes to which the students or the teacher were probably exposed, and (2) the subsequent withdrawal behavior that results. After this is completed, write a paragraph suggesting how the withdrawal behaviors can be reduced or eliminated. It is often easier to first identify the withdrawal beahviors, and then determine the conditioned aversive stimuli.

1.   Evon is in Mr. Wilkens' mathematics class. She has always done poorly in mathematics. Recently, she has ceased doing her assignments and spends much of the class period daydreaming and gazing out the window. Mr. Wilkens has just had a conference with Evon's parents. They report that they have tried to get Evon to do her mathematics homework, but have not had much success. When sent to her room to do her assignments, she does something else or sits and stares at it. When they have tried to work with her, she pouts, cries and becomes very upset.

Analyze the episode above. Label the diagram below in a manner that explains Evon's behavior. Note, you will have to speculate to some degree regarding what things are likely to be the conditioned or unconditioned stimuli.

A. _____   _____   _____
         Sc   Su --------------------- R

B. _____   _____
         Sc$_A$ --------------------- R

C. _____   _____   _____
         Sc$_A$ R   R

Suggest how the withdrawal behavior could be eliminated in the space provided below.

2.   Mr. Carey is a fifth grade teacher at West elementary. He has a reputation for being strict. For any misbehavior, he is quick to scold or use the paddle. Mr. Carey has quiet classes. Label diagram "A" below to show the learning experience to which the students have been exposed. Label diagram "B" to indicate the learning experience to which Mr. Carey has been exposed.

A.

1. _____   _____   _____
         Sc   Su   R

2. _____   _____
         Sc$_A$ -------------------- R

3. _____   _____   _____
         Sc$_A$ R,   -R

85

B.

1. _____   _____   _____
           Sc   Su   R

2. _____   _____
        Sc$_A$ -------------------- R

3. _____   _____   _____
        Sc$_A$ R,   -R

Suggest how the withdrawal behavior can be reduced or eliminated in the space provided below.

3.   Mr. Washington has just finished giving his students in biology their mid-term. He was very disappointed in their apparent low level of achievement. On the following day, he scolded the class for being the laziest class he has ever had in 10 years of teaching.

Label diagram "A" below to show the learning experience to which the students have been exposed. Label diagram "B" to indicate the learning experience to which Mr. Washington has been exposed. Hint: How is Mr. Washington defending his ego? What strengthens this behavior?

A.

1. _____   _____   _____
           Sc   Su   R

2. _____   _____
        Sc$_A$ -------------------- R

3. _____   _____   _____
        Sc$_A$ R,   -R

B.

1. _____   _____   _____
           Sc   Su   R

2. _____   _____
        Sc$_A$ -------------------- R

3. _____   _____   _____
        Sc$_A$ R,   -R

Suggest how the withdrawal behaviors of Mr. Washington and his students could be reduced or eliminated in the space provided below.

4. Frank told his English teacher that he wasn't going to do any work, "I don't care if you give me an 'F'", he informed her. The English teacher was not sure how to proceed with Frank. She knows that he is capable of doing work. Frank recently became a member of the "tough" school crowd.

Analyze the episode above. Label the diagram below in a manner that explains Frank's behavior. Suggest how you would go about changing the withdrawal behavior. Do you think low grades still cause Frank anxiety? What part does the "tough" crowd play?

A. _____   _____   _____
           Sc   Su   R

B. _____   _____
          Sc_A -------------------- R

C. _____   _____   _____
          Sc_A R,   -R

5. Jeff conceived of himself as being very bright. The aptitude and achievement test scores confirm that he is bright. His daily grades and test scores in subject matter areas, however, are low. One day after he had done poorly on a test, the other students teased him. The teacher heard him respond, "So what! I never studied for the test."

Analyze the episode above. Label the diagram below in a manner that explains Jeff's behavior. How could not studying reduce anxiety? How would you change Jeff's behavior?

A. _____   _____   _____
           Sc   Su   R

B. _____   _____
          Sc_A -------------------- R

C. (_____)   _____   _____
          Sc_A R,   -R

87

Below are four possible occurrences: As things now stand, which is the only occurrence that would cause Jeff anxiety?

    1.   He studies, and gets a good grade.
    2.   He studies and fails.
    3.   He does not study, and gets a good grade.
    4.   He does not study, and fails.

References

Bower, G. H., & Hilgard, E. R. (1981). Theories of learning. Englewood Cliffs, NJ: Prentice-Hall.

Gagne, R. M. (1985). The conditions of learning and theories of instruction. New York: Holt, Rinehart & Winston.

Skinner, B. F. (1953). Science and human behavior. New York: The Macmillan Publishing Co.

Skinner, B. F. (1971). Beyond freedom and dignity. New York: Bantam Books, Inc.

Skinner, B. F. (1973, April). The free and happy student. Educational Digest

Sulzer-Azaroff, B., & Mayer, R. G. (1986). Achieving educational excellence. New York: Holt, Rinehart & Winston.

EVALUATING OUR AFFECTIVE INSTRUCTION

Behavioral Objectives for Chapter 4

When you have completed this chapter, you should be able to recognize:

1. the relationship between affective goals and affective objectives.

2. the contribution that evaluation makes to affective instruction.

3. recognize the three stages of evaluation and their function.

4. the ultimate goal in the attainment of any affective objective.

5. the benefits to be gained from having the students keep their own records.

6. affective objectives that are best evaluated by the students.

7. when affective obejctives are stated in such a way that they are measurable.

8. how behaviors become self-reinforcing.

Discovering the Problem

As a group or in small groups, re-examine the affective objectives you derived after Chapter 1, and attempt to answer the following questions regarding them.

How would you know whether or not you had attained the objectves?
How would they be measured?
Who would measure them?
Ultimately, you would want these behaviors to become self-reinplorcing. How would you accomplish this?
How would you know if they had become self-reinforcing?
What other important function does the evaluation process perform in addition to letting you know whether or not the objective has been attained?

Successful affective instruction requires an effective evaluation system. This is the fourth step in the model of the educational act. We must be able to make valid judgments regarding the effect we are having on our students.

The evaluation of affective instructions consists of finding ways to determine if we are making the behavior changes specified in our affective objectives. Based on

these changes, we then make inferences regarding the attainment of our affective goals. If we have done an adequate job of reducing our affective goals to specific behaviors, the additive result of the attainment of our specific affective objectives should be the attainment of our general affective goals.

The evaluation of the attainment of the specific affective objectives does two things for us. First, it allows us to judge the effectiveness of our learning experiences, and second, the feedback that we acquire as the result of the evaluation provides the reinforcement we need to keep our positive approaches going.

We must be able to evaluate the effectiveness of the learning experiences we provide if we are to be successful in attaining our affective objectives. Without feedback regarding the changes that are or are not occurring in student behavior, we have no basis on which to evaluate the learning experiences we devise for our students. Well-constructed specific objectives make explicit the criteria for judging the effectiveness of the learning experiences. The learning experiences can be judged successful if they result in either the strengthening of the desired responses or the weakening of the undesired responses. Evaluative feedback that indicates that these changes are not occurring suggests a need to devise new learning experiences.

The data we get back as a result of evaluating the attainment of our objectives tend to be reinforcing for us. We need reinforcement too, and the primary source of reinforcement for us comes from being able to see that we are making progress toward attaining our objectives. This feedback provides us with a feeling of accomplishment and encourages us to go on and continue to improve the learning experiences.

The data that are collected for the purpose of evaluating the attainment of affective objectives concern with increases or decreases in the frequency or duration of the behaviors specified in the objectives. The difficulties encountered in collecting the data differ depending upon whether the data are to be collected by us or the students, and whether the data are derived from observing individual students or the entire class.

The Three Stages of Evaluating Affective Instruction

There are three stages involved in the evaluation of affective objecties. The three stages--the base rate, the treatment, and follow-up--are present in the evaluation of any affective objective. We gather data regarding frequency or duration of the behavior in each of the three stages. The data are then incorporated into a graph that provides the information we need to make judgments regarding the attainment of the objective.

Base rate data are gathered prior to the implementation of any learning experience designed to alter the frequency or duration of a behavior. The base rate is the starting point. The affective objectives indicate that a behavior is to increase or decrease in either frequency or duration. The point from which the behavior is to increase or decrease is the base rate. If there is no change in the frequency or duration of the behavior from the base rate through the treatment stage, we cannot infer that the learning experience was successful.

The treatment stage corresponds to the implementation of the learning experiences which are designed to increase or decrease the frequency or duration of the specific behavior. The evaluation during the treatment stage provides us with the data used to judge the effectiveness of the learning experiences. If the data collected during the treatment stage show that desired behaviors are being strengthened and undesired behaviors are being weakened, the learning experience is continued. If the data that are collected during this period show that either no change is occurring or a change is occurring in the wrong direction, the learning experience is altered in an attempt to insure the attainment of the objective. In this manner, changes in the learning experiences are based on objective data.

The follow-up stage comes after the treatment stage. The purpose of the follow-up stage is to help us determine if the behavior maintains itself at an acceptable level after the termination of the treatment. The ultimate goal for which we are striving is to have (1) the desired behavior specified in our affective objectives become as self-reinforcing as possible, and (2) the undesired behaviors remain at the diminished level. It is probably not accurate to say that the behaviors ever become entirely self-reinforcing. It is probably more correct to say that the maintenance of the behavior requires only occasional reinforcement. Even the strongest behaviors have to be reinforced by others occasionally or they tend toward extinction. The follow-up stage involves a return to a condition in which no planned or systematic reinforcement of the behavior occurs. The behavior may, however, be reinforced occasionally. The main idea is that the follow-up stage should resemble as closely as possible normal classroom conditions. If the behavior maintains itself at an appropriate level in the absence of the treatment, we are justified in inferring that the behavior has become self-reinforcing, and that the objective has been achieved. However, if during the follow-up stage the behavior tends to return to the pretreatment level, the treatment must be reinstated, and maintained for a duration long enough to insure that the behavior maintains itself.

Below are sample graphs of the kind that teachers can use in recording the base rate, treatment, and follow-up data.

Rules for Evaluating Our Affective Instruction

Rule 1: Continue to collect the classroom management data that are currently being collected.

We are currently collecting extensive data on classroom management objectives concerned with getting to class on time, absences, handing in assignments, etc. These data are already being gathered and recorded in the gradebook by most of us. All that remains to be done is to determine if these behaviors have increased or decreased as a result of our attempts to change them. This is usually done by comparing the percentage of students in the class performing the behaviors prior to the reinforcement of the behavior with the percentage of students performing the behaviors after the reinforcement procedures have occurred.

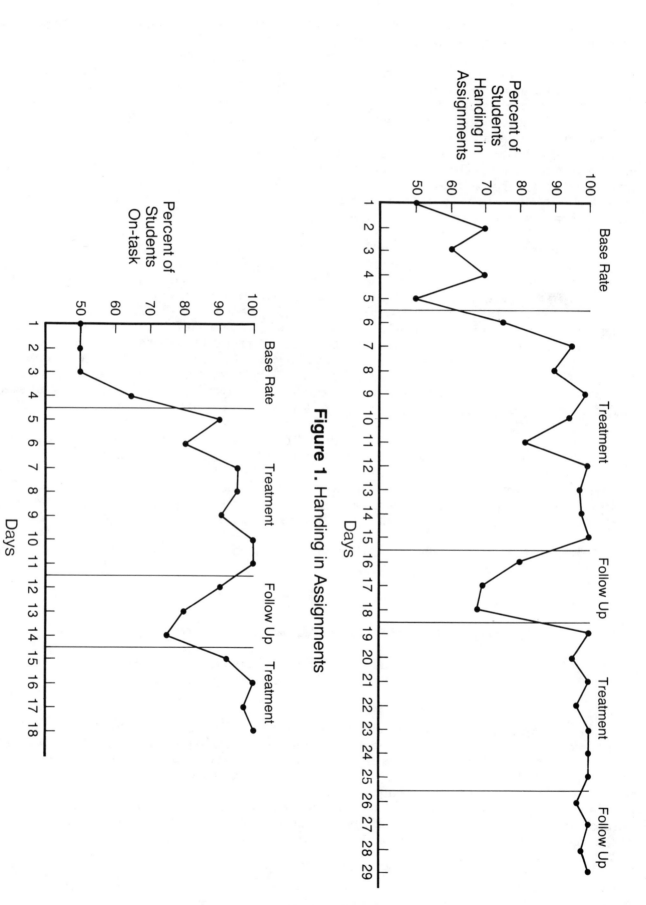

Figure 1. Handing in Assignments

Figure 2. On-task Behavior

Rule 2: Use frequency counts to evaluate student behaviors that occur during discussions.

Data can also be collected on such classroom management objectives as raising the hand and waiting to be acknowledged before answering questions and shouting-out by taking simple frequency counts. This can be done by making a mark each time the behavior occurs. The resulting data can then be compared before and after attempts at the systematic reinforcement of the behaviors.

Rule 3: Use a sampling procedure for gathering data on on-task, off-task, and disruptive behaviors of the entire class.

We are sometimes concerned with attaining objectives involved with disruption or on-task and off-task behaviors of the entire class. The data related to the attainment of these objectives can be collected by using a sampling procedure in which the student behaviors are recorded at various times before and after the beginning of treatment. The data are gathered by an observer who observes each student in a systematic fashion for ten seconds and records data regarding whether the student was disruptive, on-task or off-task. The observation can proceed from seat to seat or from work area to work area. The point is that the observation must be systematic. Every student must be equally represented in the observations. The data are then recorded, and it is possible to determine the percentage of the students in the class who are disruptive, on-task or off-task at any given time. The data should be gathered at several different times both before and after treatment in order to attain a reliable measure of the behaviors. The percentage of students in the different categories before and after the treatment phase can then be used as a basis for making inferences about the success of the reinforcement procedures used.

Rule 4: Have the students keep their own records.

We should use students to collect the data regarding the attainment of the objectives whenever possible. There are three reasons for this.

The first reason for having the students keep their own records is because we usually do not have time to keep the records. We have large numbers of students who are working toward the attainment of many different goals. We do not have the time to keep all of these records ourselves. However, we can monitor the record keeping of the students. This process is much less time consuming.

The second reason for having the students gather and record the data is because it is through gathering and recording the data that students receive their feedback. This feedback is an important reinforcer of the behaviors. Recorded data that let the students know they are making progress toward their goal is reinforcing. It tends to increase the frequency of duration with which these behaviors are performed. In addition, involving the students in the process of gathering data that indicates that they are making progress toward attaining their goals, greatly increases the frequency with which the students are reinforced. This increase in the frequency of reinforcement is an important step toward having the behaviors become self-reinforcing.

The third reason for having the students keep their own records is because the data on many of the behaviors that directly relate to continued student growth can best be collected by the students. Many of these behaviors are behaviors that occur outside of class or are behaviors that involve internalized processes. The students are often in a better position than we are to collect data on the frequency with which they examine new ideas, pursue ideas in depth, and attempt to relate new material to the outside world. They are also often the only ones capable of monitoring the frequency or duration with which they think negative thoughts about themselves or attempt to identify and avoid stimulus situations that are antecedents of undesired behaviors.

Rule 5:   Reinforce the students for keeping their own records.

Our task in evaluating our affective objectives is made easier if we can get the students to keep their own records. This does two things for us. First, it simplifies our record keeping, and second, it increases student reinforcement by providing them with feedback. Our task, once the students are keeping their records, is to reinforce their record keeping. This should be done initially on a continuous, and then on an intermittent reinforcement schedule. The use of the continuous reinforcement schedule insures that the record keeping will be established. The change of the reinforcement schedule from continuous to intermittent makes it easier for us to maintain the reinforcement for the duration necessary for the behaviors to become self-reinforcing.

Summary

The systematic attainment of our affective goals requires that we be able to evaluate the attainment of our specific affective objectives. If we do not have an adequate means of evaluating the attainment of the objectives, we have no means of judging the effectiveness of our learning experiences and consequently, no way of systematically improving our affective instruction.

The process of evaluating the attainment of our affective objectives is important because the evaluative data provide feedback which tend to be reinforcing for both us and our students. This feedback tends to reinforce us for using the procedures that have led to the attainment of the affective objectives. In addition, it reinforces the student behaviors that have led to success in attaining the objectives.

Students should be encouraged to keep their own records. There are three reasons for this. First, they should be encouraged to keep their own records because this greatly reduces our record keeping task. Second, they should keep their own records because the feedback they receive during the process tends to be reinforcing. The third reason they should be involved in the record keeping is because they are the only ones who can collect the data related to the attainment of many of our most important objectives.

The process of evaluating the attainment of the affective objectives is done in three steps. These steps consist of 1) determining the base-rate, the frequency, or duration of the behaviors prior to any intervention; (2) determining the changes in the behaviors that occur during the treatment; and 3) determining what happens to the frequency or duration of the behaviors during the follow-up period after treatment. If the behavior returns to its original level during the follow-up, the treatment is reinstated until the behavior is maintained during follow-up.

Practice Excercise 4

Read the questions below, and see if you can answer them.

1. Why does good teaching depend on good evaluation? What are positive evaluation procedures, and how would they differ from negative evaluation procedures?

2. How does the record keeping procedure tend to insure that the desired behaviors become self-reinforcing?

3. How does the evaluation system increase the frequency of reinforcement in the classroom?

4. What are our tasks when the students keep their own records?

5. To what degree do you think that cheating would be a problem if the students keep their own records? What do you think is the main factor that determines the amount of cheating? How important is this factor if we are using a positive approach based on reinforcement?

References

Buckley, N. K., & Walker, H. M. (1970). Modifying classroom behavior. Champaign, IL: Research Press.

Givner, A., & Graubard, P. (1974). A handbook of behavior modification for the classroom. New York: Holt, Rinehart, and Winston.

CHAPTER 5

IMPLEMENTING OUR AFFECTIVE INSTRUCTION

Behavioral Objectives for Chapter 5

When you have finished this chapter, you should be able to:

1. identify the major problems in using reinforcement to obtain affective objectives.

2. define positive, negative, and punitive classrooms in terms of reinforcement and punishment.

3. recognize why students perform in positive, negative and permissive classrooms.

4. given teacher statements, recognize the ones that involve the "punitive or permissive" assumption.

5. recognize the relationships between size and frequency of reinforcement in bringing about changes in behavior.

6. discriminate between positive and negative approaches, and recognize why it is difficult to be positive.

7. recognize the things that teachers do that increase or decrease their ability to reinforce through personal attention.

8. given teacher actions, identify the signal learning episodes that are likely to occur.

9. recognize the conditions that are likely to lead to the "Did you see what I did to the teacher today" syndrome.

10. identify problems associated with the attainment of affective objectives.

11. recognize the things teachers can do to increase the <u>frequency</u> of reinforcement in the classroom.

12. recognize the problems involved with attaining an adequate <u>distribution</u> of reinforcement in the classroom.

13. recognize the nature and purpose of task cards.

14. recognize the characteristics of positive evaluation systems.

15. recognize the characteristics and function of a reinforcement system.

As a group or in small groups, react to the following by attempting to answer the questions.

A careful consideration of the previous chapters implies that we can attain our affective objectives. However, to attain them we must control the signal and operant learning that goes on in our classrooms. Is it possible for us to control the signal learning and operant learning? What do we have to do to control the positive and negative signal learning experiences in our classrooms? An analysis of the previous chapters indicates that teachers, who have up to 150 different students each day, should 1) establish appropriate objectives for each student, and 2) reinforce each student on an appropriate schedule for each successive approximation of the desired goal. Is this possible? "Why" or "Why not?" What mitigating circumstances do you see? What implications does the controlling of signal and operant learning have for the use of punishment? If we cannot use punishment for controlling student behavior, what is the alternative? What generally happens when we lose our ability to reinforce through the use of personal attention?

We Need to Establish Positive Schools

The attainment of our affective goals requires that we establish positive schools and classrooms (Skinner, 1953). Affective goals concerned with developing positive self-concepts, self-directedness, self-motivation, as well as appreciations of nature, literature, art, music, etc., cannot be attained in negative or permissive schools. The attainment of goals such as these require a planned, systematic approach that is based on positive reinforcement. The goals cannot be attained in a punitive atmosphere in which the frequent use of punishment creates signal learning experiences that tend to turn learning and learning related activities into anxiety provoking stimuli. Nor can the goals be attained in a laissez faire atmosphere in which affective learning is left to occur in an incidental fashion.

The attainment of our affective goals requires that we establish positive classrooms. Positive classrooms are classrooms in which students perform their learning tasks in order to attain either extrinsic reinforcement (reinforcement from others) or intrinsic (self) reinforcement. The primary characteristic of the positive classroom is the frequent and intelligent use of positive reinforcement to increase the frequency and duration of desired behaviors.

Positive, rather than negative or permissive, classrooms are required to facilitate the attainment of positive goals. The concepts of "positive," "negative," and "permissive" classrooms are characteristically used in an arbitrary fashion. It is possible, however, to define the concepts in terms of the ways in which reinforcement and punishment are used.

Positive classrooms are classrooms in which the students perform learning tasks in order to attain intrinsic or extrinsic reinforcement.

Negative classrooms are classrooms in which the students perform learning tasks in order to avoid the aversive consequences of not performing them.

Permissive classrooms are classrooms in which the teacher is neither punitive nor positive. With a permissive approach, the reinforcement within the classroom comes to reside with class members, and they select which behaviors are and are not going to be reinforced.

Positive affective objectives can seldom be attained in a negative classroom. This is especially true of the important objectives in which we indicate a desire that our students go on and continue to learn long after they have left the classroom. It has often been pointed out that schools are primarily negative institutions (Skinner, 1973). Schools are negative institutions to the extent that students are performing their learning tasks in order to avoid the aversive consequences of not performing them. They are negative to the extent that students:

> study in order to avoid failing.
> hand in assignments in order to avoid a low grade.
> come to class on time in order to avoid detention.
> remain quiet in order to avoid criticism.
> attend school in order to avoid punishment.

There are many other examples that can be used to illustrate the negative approaches found in our schools. The problem occurs because it is difficult to instill in students a desire to learn and grow in such an environment. Negative approaches are more likely to promote avoidance behaviors that are incompatible with the behavior specified in our positive objectives than to create self-motivated, self-directed students.

Permissive classrooms are also unlikely to lead to the attainment of our positive affective goals. Permissive classrooms are neither punitive nor positive. In permissive classrooms, we neither reinforce desired behavior nor punish undesired behavior. The consequence of this situation is that the peer group comes to control the reinforcement in the classroom. They then select which behaviors are and are not to be reinforced. The problem is that the behaviors they reinforce usually are disruptive, and nearly always incompatible with the attainment of our objectives.

Positive approaches to both learning and classroom control are often overlooked. There seems to be an assumption in education that we must be either "punitive" or "permissive". The reasoning seems to be that if teachers are having trouble controlling their class, it is because they have been too permissive. They are letting the students get away with too much, and are not "making" the students "toe the mark" and learn. This reasoning leads to the next obvious step. If the teacher got in trouble as a result of being too permissive, then the solution is to be punitive—get tough. What is overlooked in this process is that we do not have to be either punitive or permissive. We can be positive, and use positive reinforcement as the means for attaining our goals.

Our Task in Implementing Affective Instruction

Our task in designing learning experiences to lead to the attainment of our affective objectives consists of finding ways to reinforce each student on an appropriate schedule for each successive approximation of the desired behaviors. The task is complex because each student is typically in a different position in regard to the attainment of any given objective. Some students may have already attained the objective while others have yet to make a beginning. In addition, some students require reinforcement on a continuous schedule before progress can be made toward the attainment of the objective, while other students require only intermittent reinforcement. The attainment of the objectives requires that we recognize these individual differences, find the necessary reinforcers, stimulate the desired behaviors and appropriately reinforce the behaviors.

Broadly stated, our problems in attaining our affective goals center around finding ways of (1) providing the frequency, variety, and distribution of reinforcement necessary; and (2) controlling the peer reinforcement that occurs in the classroom. A discussion of these problems follows. The discussion is concerned primarily with pointing out the difficulties in attaining the necessary reinforcement. A more detailed solution to the problems of acquiring needed reinforcement is presented in later chapters.

Problems Concerned with the Practicality of Reinforcing Each Student for Each Successive Approximation of a Desired Behavior

At first glance, the task of reinforcing each student for each small step toward a goal appears to be impossible. To many of us, who have up to 150 different students each day, the task of reinforcing each of them for every step toward a goal appears overwhelming. The mere mention of the task conjures up images of a teacher on roller skates racing about the room popping M & M candies into the open mouths of the waiting students. Those of us with this perspective are quick to point out that if we attempted to provide the needed reinforcement to all students we would have time for nothing else.

The problem indicated above centers about the attainment of an adequate frequency and distribution of reinforcement. The solution to the problem requires that we move away from the traditional classroom and toward the individualization of instruction. The task of acquiring the frequency and distribution of reinforcement needed for attaining the objectives is impossible in the traditional classroom where students are treated as though they are all functioning at the same level. Solving the problem requires that instruction be individualized by assigning appropriate objectives to each student. Even then, acquiring the needed frequency and distribution of reinforcement would be impossible if it were not for some extenuating circumstances.

The problem of providing the needed frequency of reinforcement is simplified because few students need to be reinforced for every move they make in the direction of the affective goal. Most students are already on an intermittent reinforcement schedule. We can expect that the longer students are exposed to positive approaches, the less frequently they will need to be reinforced. Ultimately, we are attempting to develop students who are self-reinforcing, and the more successful we are in attaining this goal, the less frequently we will need to reinforce the students.

We can also greatly increase the frequency and distribution of reinforcement by establishing individual and group reinforcement systems. The use of reinforcement systems allows us to increase reinforcement by creating conditions under which many small reinforcers can be accumulated and used to acquire one large reinforcer. In addition, it is possible for us to create group reinforcement systems which will result in class members reinforcing each other for attaining academically desirable goals. The harnessing of peer reinforcement creates a situation in which the frequency of reinforcement tends to go up geometrically, while at the same time, the distribution of reinforcement among the students is automatically extended.

Problems Concerned with Creating the Conditions So That
Each Student Receives Adequate Reinforcement

Two other problems we encounter during affective instruction suggest aspects of the distribution problem. We point out that it is very difficult to find an opportunity to reinforce some students. This is because when we do establish agreements with these students, the task is not accomplished and we have no opportunity to reinforce them.

The problem arises because of conditions that exist in the traditional classroom. Reinforcement in traditional classrooms not only does not occur frequently enough, the reinforcement that does occur is not adequately distributed. A disproportionate amount of the reinforcement goes to the more able students. The individual differences in ability within the classroom result in a situation where many low-ability students are not able to attain many of the cognitive and psychomotor objectives that we establish. This creates conditions under which these students receive little or no reinforcement.

We can solve the problem by designing educational objectives that are appropriate for each student regardless of ability level. If the goals we set are appropriate for the student, the student will be able to make progress toward the attainment of the objective, and we will be able to reinforce the behaviors that led to the progress. The creation of conditions so that each student can be reinforced requires that we establish goals only slightly above the current level of the students. Under these conditions, the students will be able to make progress toward the desired behaviors, and we will be able to adequately distribute the reinforcement to all students.

Problems Concerned with the Availability of the
Necessary Reinforcers in the Schools

Another practical objection that we often raise is based on the notion that the necessary reinforcers are not available in the schools. We point out that while stars, smiling faces, etc., are good reinforcers for small children, they are not appropriate for older students. Older children, we suggest, require larger reinforcers which neither we nor the school systems can afford.

Those of us who raise this objection are making a common error. What we generally fail to realize is that the frequency of reinforcement is a more important variable than size or cost of reinforcers in changing behavior. Many of us have not had much trouble finding the reinforcers necessary for attaining our objectives. The situation is somewhat different in each school, but if we look around and utilize our imagination, we can find a large variety of reinforcers in the classroom, school, community, and surrounding area. A careful observation of the behavior of students will also help us identify still other potential reinforcers.

The attainment of the necessary variety of reinforcers is made easier because:

> nearly anything that increases student freedom or adds variety to the school day is reinforcing.

> we are currently giving away many large reinforcers. These can be used to create reinforcement systems which will allow us to reinforce individual students many times on the way to attaining the larger reinforcer.

> an analysis of student behaviors also yields clues to potential reinforcers. If we analyze current student behaviors to determine the reinforcers that are maintaining them, we can then use these same reinforcers to strengthen other desired behaviors.

Problems Concerned with Countering the Peer-Group Reinforcement of Undesired Behaviors

A second problem in implementing our affective instruction occurs because the peer-group often reinforces behaviors that are incompatible with the behaviors we are seeking to strengthen. While our smiles, praise and attention are good reinforcers for children in grade school, they are not necessarily reinforcing for students in the upper grades. Beginning with adolescence, peer-group reinforcement has as much or more influence on student behavior than teacher attention. This influence is often used to counter our attempts to reinforce desired student behaviors.

It is true that the importance of the peer group to the individual does increase with age. The objection, however, carries with it a certain inevitability, and ignores our ability to modify classroom conditions.

The increased ability of the peer-group to reinforce its members does not necessarily mean a corresponding reduction in our ability to attain our objectives. An increase in the ability of the peer-group to reinforce its members means a reduction in our ability to attain affective objectives only if our goals differ from those of the peer-group. If an adversary relationship is allowed to develop in which the goals of the peer-group and our goals are incompatible, the peer-group will reinforce behaviors that are incompatible, with our objectives. However, if classroom conditions can be developed in such a way that the goals of the peer-group correspond with the goals we have established, the peer-group will reinforce individual class members for the attainment of these goals.

Practice Exercise 5-1

Read the questions that follow, and see if you can think of ways of solving the problems.

1. Roosevelt Junior High School has a bad reputation. Student behavior is so bad that teacher turnover is high. The school has just hired a new principal, and he has called a meeting of the teachers and concerned citizens to discuss the actions that need to be taken. Below is a list of suggested actions.

    We need to get tougher. The teachers need to have the backing of the administration and parents.

    We have to have improved discipline. The teachers cannot let the students run the school. They have to take charge and be strict.

    When I went to school, they made us work. You have to make the students work.

    The school needs to set up a detention room for troublemakers. Then if students misbehave, we can get them out of the classroom.

    We need to establish hall and restroom monitors to stop the trouble that erupts before and between classes.

    There are many other suggestions of the same type. Explain why the suggestions put forth are all largely negative. What assumption is involved?

2. At an inservice workshop at Wentworth High School the speaker suggested that it should be possible for every student to take home a positive report card. The statement brought the following reaction from some of the teachers.

    We are preparing our students to take their place in a competitive world. If you create a school situation in which all students take home positive report cards, you are just deluding the students.

    How would you respond to this comment?

3. The peer-group often reinforces undesired behaviors that are incompatible with our goals. Can you think of examples of this? What can we do to overcome the situation?

4. Mr. Straw, a new teacher, is having trouble controlling his class. He discussed the problem with his friend, Mr. Martin. Mr. Martin told him that the problem was that he was letting the kids get away with too much, and that he had to make them behave. What assumptions regarding classroom control has Mr. Martin made? What other alternative has he overlooked?

5. It has been suggested that our task in attaining affective goals is to reinforce each student for each successive approximation of the desired goal. Is this a correct statement of the problem? Why or why not? How would you state the problem? Is a solution to the problem possible? Why or why not?

6. Can we achieve an adequate distribution of reinforcement to all students? Why is it a difficult problem, and how can it be overcome?

7. Are the reinforcers necessary for attaining our objectives available? Why or why not?

Improving Our Ability to Reinforce

The attainment of the ne essary frequency and distribution of reinforcement for attaining our affective goals will be easier if we establish ourselves as good reinforcing agents. We are the primary source of reinforcement in the classroom, and our smiles, attention and feedback are among the most readily available reinforcers. All of us, however, do not have the same ability to reinforce our students. One of the most common errors we make in attempting to attain our positive objectives is to think that we have reinforced a behavior when it has not been reinforced. We need to remember that if the "reinforcers" do not strengthen the behaviors they follow, they cannot be deemed reinforcers. Our personal attention is likely to strengthen student behavior only if there is rapport between us and the student. Our ability to reinforce students, however, is not fixed, and we need to take every action possible to increase our ability to reinforce students through personal attention. There are four rules that we can follow that will increase our ability to reinforce through personal attention.

Rules for Improving Our Ability to Reinforce

Rule 1: Be positive.

Our ability to reinforce through personal attention increases as we come to rely on positive rather than negative approaches. The more effective we become in the use of positive reinforcement and positive signal learning experiences, the better reinforcing agents we become. Unfortunately, the opposite is also true. The more we come to rely on negative approaches to modify student behavior, the less likely it is that we will be able to use personal attention to strengthen desired behaviors. The use of negative approaches sets in motion signal learning experiences which tend to cause us to become conditioned aversive stimuli, and limit our ability to reinforce through personal attention.

We sometimes unwittingly create a series of classroom learning experiences which not only cause us to lose our ability to reinforce our students, but actually create a situation where students begin reinforcing each other for making our lives miserable. This behavior generally occurs because we (1) have alienated a large part of the class through negative methods of control and evaluation, and (2) are not strong enough physically or psychologically to control the students through the use of punishment. The situation is most likely to occur with older students. When we make excessive use of negative approaches such as group punishment and punitive grading, the reinforcement in the classroom tends to come to reside largely with the peer group. The usual outcome is what can be called the "Did you see what I did to the teacher" syndrome. This syndrome of behaviors occurs when students begin reinforcing each other for various kinds of disruptive behaviors. The result of this syndrome of behaviors is that many of us end up looking for another line of work.

The situation described above can be avoided if we will learn to "Think Positively." Thinking positively is difficult. It is not only difficult for us, but

109

it is difficult for everyone. We have been conditioned to be negative to the point where it takes a conscious effort for most of us to think positively. The author once visited a school in which teachers were attempting to implement a school-wide positive approach to instruction. One of the things that the teachers continually commented about was the difficulty they encountered in attempting to stay positive. This fact was attested to by the large numbers of signs distributed about the school in which they admonished themselves to "Think Positive."

Thinking positively requires that we focus our attention on reinforcing those things the students are doing right, rather than on punishing those things they are doing wrong. There are three main reasons why we must make a conscious effort to be positive. First, we have all to a greater or lesser degree been reinforced for punishing, and the tendency to punish is strong. Second, undesired behavior typically does not occur as frequently in the classroom as desired behavior. For this reason, it is easy to ignore desired behaviors by treating them as something the students ought to do anyway. Third, we tend to teach the way we were taught and, unfortunately, the schools most of us attended were largely negative institutions. We performed in order to avoid the aversive consequences of not performing. Thus, the models that we tend to imitate are negative.

Some examples of positive and negative approaches to the same task are listed below. A cursory examination of these statements can help us recognize the pervasiveness of the negative approach. Unfortunately, the negative statements are the rule rather than the exception. We need to increase our positive statements, and reduce our negative statements.

Task A

> The negative approach--If you do not study, you will have additional homework.

> The positive approach--If you study quietly for 15 minutes, you can talk quietly for 5 minutes at the end of the period.

Task B

> The negative approach--If your paper is not neat, 10 points will be subtracted from your grade.

> The positive approach--If you hand in a neat paper, 10 points will be added to your grade.

Task C

> The negative approach--If your assignments are not done by Thursday, you will automatically lose 10 points on your grade on the project.

> The positive approach--If your project is done by Thursday, you will have 10 bonus points added to your grade.

Notice that in the situations above the end result in terms of where the student is in the distribution of grades, etc. is likely to be the same with both approaches. The student response, however, to the learning task tends to be considerably different. Students perform differently when they are working to get a higher grade or bonus points than they do when they are trying to avoid the lower grade or loss of points. Students work harder and feel better about it when positive approaches are used.

Rule 2: Associate yourself with positive signal learning experiences.

The problems mentioned above will not occur if teachers design learning experiences which result in positive reinforcement and positive signal learning experience. The more teachers reinforce and associate themselves with positive signal learning experiences, the better reinforcers they become, and the easier it is for them to attain their positive motivational objectives.

Rule 3: Talk to students about their interests.

Talking to students individually about their interests and hobbies is an excellent way for us to increase our ability to reinforce through personal attention. The approach yields the best results if discussions take place prior to the time that we have encountered any discipline problems with the student. We characteristically talk to students primarily about school-related topics; and when we talk to them about their interests, we tend to create a special situation which increases rapport and enhances our ability to reinforce.

Rule 4: Send positive reports home.

Sending home positive reports on student behavior or progress is a good way of increasing our ability to reinforce, as well as enlisting parental support to help in the attainment of educational objectives. We often have to do so e searching in order to find positive things to say about some students. However, once appropriate, attainable objectives have been specified and reinforced, making positive reports becomes easier. We often lament that we never get a chance to talk to the parents with whom "we really need to talk." The parents who attend parent-teacher conferences seem to always be the ones who have children with few problems. This situation arises because the parents "we really need to see" have never been reinforced and have often been punished for attending parent-teacher conferences. Consequently, the behavior of attending the conferences has been extinguished. The parents who attend the conferences are typically those who have been reinforced by the news that their children are doing well. The act of sending positive reports home which point out the behaviors on which the student is making progress can help remedy the problem.

Positive reports that indicate the progress the student is making toward attaining specific goals are reinforcing rather than threatening to parents. In addition, they directly suggest ways in which the parents can help us achieve mutual goals.

1. You are talking to Mr. French, a new teacher, in the school lounge. Mr. French relates the following:

   I don't know what happened. I always wanted to be a friend of my students. I tried to get them to like me and accept me as one of them. Now I feel that they are taking advantage of me. They seem to do pretty much whatever they want, and when I try to make them do their work they ignore me.

   What kind of classroom has developed? Use the concepts of reinforcement to explain (1) what has occurred in the situation above, and (2) what Mr. French needs to do to regain control of his class.

2. Diagram and label the signal learning experience involved in each of the following situations. What would you predict would happen to the ability of Mr. West and Ms. Colby to reinforce through the use of personal attention? What is likely to happen in terms of the support the teachers receive from parents?

   Mr. West sends a positive letter home to the parents of Fred. Fred is an underachiever.

   Ms. Colby knows that Harris is very interested in cars. She makes a point of asking questions, and talking to him about his car.

3. Diagram and label the signal learning experiences and subsequent escape behaviors the student and teacher are experiencing.

   Ms. Wren teaches ninth grade English. She got along with her students reasonably well until the end of the first grading period. The first grading period she gave most of her students "C's" and "D's" because she felt they could not do ninth grade work. She began having more discipline problems in the second term. She decided to make the students work, and responded to these problems by grading "tougher." The number of student papers and homework assignments handed in has dropped off considerably. Test scores are low. When the test grades are given to the students, they laugh and compare grades or else throw the papers into the wastepaper basket. The school counselor asked a number of the students about their low English grade, and was told by the students that this grade does not count because it's from Ms. Wren, and nobody likes her anyway. Recently, the "trouble makers" have been playing tricks on Ms. Wren, and the class has been enjoying it immensely.

4. Listed below are a number of statements made by students. Put "+" for positive and a "-" for negative after the statements depending upon whether they indicate that the school is viewed as a positive or negative institution. Tell why the statement indicates a positive or negative view.

a.   I have to do well on this test or it will lower my grade. _____

b.   If I can find the answer to this "brain teaser", I will   _____
     get 20 bonus points.

c.   If I am late for class again, I will have to go to   _____
     detention.

5.   Mr. Brown and Mr. White both have a problem with Richard disrupting their
     classes. Both teachers tell Richard to "be quiet", "sit down", and "get to work"
     in the same tone of voice. The reaction of Richard was quite different to the
     response of the teachers. His reaction to Mr. Brown was to smile, walk slowly to
     his desk and begin working. His reaction to Mr. White was to say, "Make me."
     Use the concept of reinforcement to explain why Richard reacted so differently to
     the same stimulus.

6.   You are having a discussion with Mr. Winkle, the science teacher. Mr. Winkle has
     a reputation for being punitive. During the discussion he says, "Positive
     reinforcement does not work. I tried it with my class and it did not strengthen
     the behavior." How would you answer Mr. Winkle? Diagram and label the signal
     learning experiences Mr. Winkle has been providing for his students. Why do you
     think Mr. Winkle thinks reinforcement does not work?

7.   Diagram and label the learning experiences to which the different parents have
     been exposed. Describe what needs to be done to remedy the situation.

     Mr. Wolf, the principal, has called a faculty meeting. He is disturbed because
     the parent-teacher conferences are poorly attended by parents. This, he feels,
     is keeping the school from attaining many of its objectives. During the meetings
     the teachers repeatedly lament that the only parents they ever get to see are
     those whose children are doing well. They point out that they never get to see
     the "parents the teachers really need to see."

Attaining the Necessary Reinforcement

Successful affective instruction requires that we provide a greater variety and frequency of reinforcement in our classroom. In the typical classroom the primary reinforcement is our feedback and our grades. A problem arises because even these are not necessarily reinforcing. To be reinforcers they must strengthen particular behaviors, and we are not always sure what behaviors they are strengthening. Positive feedback that indicates student responses are correct could conceivably strengthen either or both the responses the students make or the act of responding to our questions. In the typical classroom, we do not evaluate these outcomes, so we do not know. The grades that we place on student papers also may or may not be reinforcing. The grade is reinforcing only if it strengthens a behavior, and we typically do not know what behaviors our grades strengthen. There is often a considerable amount of time that lapses between student performance and receiving the grade—a condition that reduces the probability that the grades will reinforce the behavior. If we are to be successful in attaining our affective, as well as our cognitive and psychomotor, goals, we have to create classroom conditions that provide a much greater variety and frequency of reinforcement.

We need to alter our approach if we are to attain the frequency and variety of reinforcement necessary for attaining our goals. The attainment of our affective goals requires us to establish classroom conditions which allow us to follow desired student behaviors immediately with reinforcers that strengthen the behaviors. This means that we must have many and varied reinforcers immediately available. Reinforcers lose their ability to reinforce. Reinforcers that are reinforcing to one student are not necessarily reinforcing to another, and reinforcers that are reinforcing at one time are not necessarily reinforcing at another time. All of these conditions combine to complicate our problem. We cannot expect to be able to pick the needed reinforcers off the top of our head at a moment's notice. They must be available as part of the conditions we establish within the classroom.

Every school system has within it the resources necessary to provide the needed frequency and variety of reinforcement. However, the attainment of this reinforcement requires that we be creative and flexible. Below are two sets of rules that we can use to help increase 1) the variety, and 2) the frequency of reinforcement in the classroom.

Rules for Increasing the Variety of Reinforcement in the Classroom

The process of providing the students with the necessary variety of reinforcers is simplified if we develop reinforcement menus. Reinforcement menus are lists of reinforcers that we can use to strengthen desired behaviors. The availability of a reinforcement menu releases us from the problem of coming up with appropriate reinforcers on the spur of the moment. Once we have developed a reinforcement menu, all that needs to be done is to have the students select their own reinforcer from the reinforcement menu. It is often convenient to develop two or three menus with different levels of reinforcers. This allows us to equate student behavior with the appropriate reinforcer. A reinforcer from menu "A" might be selected to strengthen relatively minor behaviors; a reinforcer from menu "B" for strengthening behaviors that require more student effort; and a selection from menu "C" could be used to strengthen major student achievements. A list of potential reinforcers that have been used by others is included in the Appendix "B".

There are five basic rules we can follow that will help in constructing reinforcement menus containing a wide variety of reinforcers.

Rule 1:   Stop giving away potential reinforcers!
            Incorporate them into reinforcement menus,
            and use them to strengthen desired behavior.

We typically have a large number of reinforcers that we are giving away. These reinforcers should be placed in a reinforcement menu, and their presentation to the student made contingent on the performance of desired behaviors. The potential reinforcers that we are giving away vary, but they include such things as:

        running errands
        passing out materials
        being first in line
        selecting games to play
        putting on plays
        working on cars
        field trips

Student perceptions of our activities change once they are incorporated into the reinforcement menu and made something to be earned rather than something that is given away. Activities that are given away tend to be thought of by students as something which is owed to them. When this occurs, the students no longer identify with the activities. Students tend to identify with those activities they have to work to attain. They tend to think of earned ativities as "Our field trip," "Our dance," "Our trip to the French restaurant," etc. Conversely, activities that are given to them tend to be thought of as belonging to us or the school. It becomes "A Field trip," instead of "Our field trip." Students need goals with which to identify. We can provide these goals, while at the same time increasing the items on our reinforcement menu, by creating conditions so that the students earn those activities that are currently being given away.

Rule 2:   Observe student behaviors to determine those behaviors
            that have a high level of occurrence. These behaviors
            can be used to strengthen behaviors that have a low
            level of occurrence.

We can, by observing the kinds of behaviors or activities the students engage in during their free time, add a number of reinforcers to the reinforcement menu. The behaviors can then be used in conjunction with the Premack hypothesis to strengthen

116

other desired behaviors. The Premack hypothesis indicates that if behaviors having a low probability of occurrence are followed by behaviors that have a high probability of occurrence, the effect is to strengthen the weaker behaviors. For example, we might observe the class and note that the students like to talk to each other during the time allocated for studying. The stronger behavior, "talking," can be used to strengthen the weaker behavior, "studying." We might indicate to the students that if they studied for 15 minutes, they could talk quietly for 5 minutes. The effect would be to strengthen studying behavior.

Rule 3: Search the surrounding community for reinforcers.

The community can provide us with many reinforcers that can be added to our menus. Many of the reinforcers available in the community have the advantage of being educational as well as reinforcing. Nature outings, pollution studies, visitations to points of historical interest, demonstrations by community members, community cultural events, etc., are just a few of the many possible reinforcers available in the community. These events tend to be reinforcing because they add freedom and variety to the school day, and if we are alert we will incorporate them into our menus, and use them as a basis for strengthening desired behavior.

Rule 4: Discover how students use their free time.

We can add to our reinforcement menus by discovering how students use their free time. Individual students have hobbies, skills and other activities that are reinforcing for them. We can use these activities as a basis for strengthening other desired behaviors. For example, we can allow the student to use classroom time to work on these activities provided that they have performed other desired tasks. Students like to talk about their interests, and we can use their interests in music, hunting, fishing, cars, motorcycles, etc., to strengthen desired academic behaviors.

We can discover how the students use their free time by talking to them, observing their behavior, or by having them write papers on how they use their free time. These procedures provide us with a large number of possible reinforcers in a short time. These reinforcers can be incorporated into our menus and used to increase desired student behaviors.

Rule 5: Analyze undesired behaviors to determine what is maintaining them.

We can acquire reinforcers for our reinforcement menus by analyzing undesired behaviors to determine what is maintaining them. The same reinforcers which maintain undesired behaviors can also be used to strengthen desired behaviors. For example, if it is determined that the peer group is reinforcing the disruptive antics of a student, it is also likely peer attention would be a good reinforcer to use for strengthening desired behaviors such as coming to class on time and handing in assignments.

Rules for Increasing the Frequency of Reinforcement in the Classroom

The use of many small reinforcers causes changes in behavior that normally cannot be attained by the use of a few large or more expensive reinforcers. Most of our important affective objectives cannot be attained by exposing the student to a few large reinforcers. We are all familiar with students who start out each new grading period by turning over a new leaf. They declare that they are going to work hard, and get a good grade this term. The student ususally works hard and does better during the first part of the term only to fade at the end. The problem occurs because there is not enough reinforcement during the term, and the grade at the end of the term is too far away to maintain the behavior.

It is difficult for most of us to learn that the frequency of reinforcement is more important than the size of the reinforcer in changing behavior. It is probably difficult to learn this because the individual being reinforced does not realize that his need is for more frequent reinforcement rather than larger reinforcers. For example, workers in industry often receive large pay raises, but still remain dissatisfied and discontented in their jobs. An analysis of the situation reveals that while the workers say they want more money, what they really want is recognition of their achievements and a feeling of importance. These needs are not adequately satisfied by a pay check at the end of the month. The satisfaction of these needs depends on frequent acts of attention and recognition, and not just a large pay check at the end of the month.

There are three basic rules or procedures that we can follow that will lead to the needed increase in the frequency of reinforcement in our classrooms.

Rule 1: **Provide for feedback--involve the students in keeping their own records, and reinforce them for keeping the records.**

The frequency of reinforcement in the classroom can be increased by requiring the students to keep records of their own behavior. The records provide the students with "feedback," itself a kind of reinforcer, that lets them know how they are doing. Feedback is easier to institute into the classroom than many other kinds of reinforcement. A graph or a written report of the progress being made is a tangible artifact that both the student and the teacher see. The feedback attained from the record tends to strengthen the behavior being recorded. In addition, however, we need to reinforce the process of keeping the records if record keeping is to be maintained. Many studies attest to the importance of record keeping in changing behavior among them are (Hannum, Thoresen, & Hubbard, 1974; Stamps, 1973).

The movement from teacher reinforcement to self-reinforcement requires continuous feedback. The students need to know that progress is being made, and the desired behaviors are becoming stronger. The important thing is to let self-reinforcement take over. Self-reinforcement occurs when the students become convinced that they are growing and doing a good job. The student needs this, but where are they to get it? The internal reinforcer--the satisfaction of a job well done--needs to be corroborated and reinforced by visible recorded daily evidence that indicates the desired behavior is strengthening. The process of establishing a behavior and strengthening it until it becomes essentially self-reinforcing, requiring only occasional teacher reinforcement, appears to involve three periods. The three basic periods are: (1) a period in which frequent positive reinforcement by the teacher plus continuous feedback leads to rapid strengthening of the desired behavior; (2) a period in which infrequent positive reinforcement by the teacher is accompanied by continuous feedback; and (3) a period in which the teacher is only a very occasional source of positive reinforcement, and feedback is overwhelmingly the principal source of reinforcement. The result of the three steps is that the behaviors tend to become self-reinforcing, and there is a corresponding increase in the frequency of reinforcement in the classrooms.

Rule 2: Develop individual reinforcement systems.

We can greatly increase the frequency of reinforcement within the classroom by developing reinforcing systems for individual students. The process of developing and using reinforcement systems with individual students consists of (1) identifying a major reinforcer for which the individual is willing to work, and (2) developing a system of smaller reinforcers which can be accumulated and turned in to attain the larger reinforcer. In the situation described below, Mr. James has developed an individual reinforcement system.

> Mr. James, the principal, tells Bill, a chronic troublemaker, that he will give him 10 points each time he goes through an entire class without disrupting it, and will allow him to go swimming after he has accumulated 150 points.

In the development of a reinforcement system the large reinforcer is necessary if the small reinforcers, generally points, tokens, etc., are to continue to reinforce. In the example above, it is unlikely that Bill would be willing to work for points if it were not possible to exchange them for the major reinforcer--swimming.

The small reinforcers in the reinforcement system are essential for the establishment of a positive reinforcement system because they make possible the contiguity of reinforcement necessary to strengthen the desired behaviors. In the situation above, Mr. James is able to provide Bill with points each time he completes a class without disrupting it. The points are readily available to Mr. James, and can be presented immediately after the response has occurred, thus providing the contiguity needed for changing Bill's behavior.

The frequent use of many small reinforcers can bring about changes in behavior that normally cannot be attained by the use of a few larger or more expensive reinforcers. Mr. James is more likely to bring about the desired changes in the

119

behavior of Bill through the use of the reinforcement system, than he would if he simply offered to let Bill go swimming on Friday if he did not disrupt his classes. Most of us err in trying to bring about changes in behavior in a manner similar to Mr. Orwell below:

Mr. Orwell and Mr. Noland both have high ability, low achieving sons. They have both determined that their sons would like to have ski equipment that cost 400 dollars. Mr. Orwell tells his son that if he makes the honor roll for the semester he will buy him the equipment. Mr. Noland determines how well his son typically performs in the different academic areas, and offers to contribute one dollar toward the ski equipment every time his son's performance on daily assignments meets or exceeds a level previously attained.

In this situation it is likely that both boys will enter into the agreement with equal enthusiasm. It is likely, however, that Mr. Orwell's son will not be able to maintain his effort toward the objective. The mistake that Mr. Orwell has made is that of assuming the way to make a major change in the behavior of his son is to offer him a major reinforcer. The agreement that was established provided the son with the possibility of attaining one major reinforcer at the end of the semester which was about four months away. The agreement Mr. Noland made with his son would allow him to reinforce his son for each step along the way to the goal. Mr. Noland established an agreement that would allow him to reinforce his son as many as 400 times on the way to his goal. This situation is much more likely to result in the desired changes in the behavior of his son. Most of our important objectives cannot be attained by offering the student one major reinforcer. Instead, they require the shaping of the desired behavior by the reinforcement of successive approximations of the desired behavior. The shaping, in turn, requires the frequent presentation of smaller reinforcers rather than the presentation of a few large ones.

Rule 3: Harness peer reinforcement.

The procedures for harnessing peer reinforcement are dealt with in greater detail in Chapter 6. The harnessing of peer reinforcement is a means for greatly increasing the frequency of reinforcement in our classrooms. As long as we think of ourselves as the primary source of reinforcement in the classroom, any increase in the frequency of reinforcement tends to be largely linear. However, if we establish classroom conditions that lead to the harnessing of peer reinforcement, the frequency of reinforcement tends to increase geometrically.

Our class is just like any other group. It will reinforce individual members to the extent that they contribute to group goals. The problem arises because our classes typically have no goals with which they identify. We have generally done two things in our classrooms that have greatly reduced the frequency of peer reinforcement of desired behaviors. First, we have failed to establish goals with which the peer group can identify; and second, we have created a competitive situation in which if one student wins the other loses. These conditions need to be rectified if we are to increase the frequency of peer reinforcement in our classrooms. More specifically, we need to establish major goals with which the peer group can identify; and then use the major goal to create classroom conditions in which if one student wins--they all win. Under these conditions the frequency of reinforcement of desired behaviors in our classrooms will increase greatly.

Practice Exercise 5-3

1. Listed below are a number of statements that have been taken out of context. Place an "F" after each statement if the statement would support an argument for why teachers <u>can</u> provide the frequency of reinforcement necessary for attaining their affective objectives in the classroom. Place an "A" after each statement if the statement would support an argument for why teachers <u>cannot</u> provide the necessary frequency of reinforcement for attaining their affective objectives.

   a. I have 150 different students each day.
   _____

   b. Most students do not need constant teacher attention. They usually work all right by themselves.
   _____

   c. Finding out that your response is correct is reinforcing.
   _____

   d. Keeping records of where each student is in relationship to a given goal is impossible.
   _____

   e. Teachers have to teach subject matter too.
   _____

   f. Keeping records of your progress is reinforcing.
   _____

   g. I cannot be everywhere at once.
   _____

   h. My ultimate goal is that the students become "self-reinforcing."
   _____

   i. The peer-group either ignores or is critical of the achievements of individual students.
   _____

   j. The peer group has no goals related to academic success.
   _____

   k. The peer group will support individuals who contribute to the goals of the group.
   _____

   l. The peer group is willing to work for nearly any goal that adds freedom and variety to the school day.
   _____

   m. The peer group reinforces behaviors that are inconsistent with the goals of the teacher.
   _____

   n. Teachers have many potential reinforcers they are currently giving away.
   _____

   o. Teachers can construct reinforcement systems in which many small reinforcers can be accumulated to make possible the attainment of a large reinforcer.
   _____

   p. Good students are already self-motivated.
   _____

2. Ms. Glass has just been assigned to teach a new remedial English class. The class as a whole has experienced very little academic success. The result of this is that students are not motivated. Ms. Glass decides to develop a positive contract with the class in an attempt to increase their effort. She makes the following contract which was agreed to by the class:

   If the class will increase the percentage of assignments handed in to 90 percent by the end of the current grading period, they can take a field trip to a play that is being presented in a nearby town.

   Would you expect the contract to produce the desired results? Why or why not?

3. The class begs Mr. Briggs to let them put on a play. After they had begged for three weeks, he relented and allowed them to put on the play.

   What error has he made?
   What behavior was reinforced?
   What should Mr. Briggs have done?

4. Ms. Webster's class has decided that they want to go on a field trip. After the students had begged for a week, Ms. Webster relented and allowed them to go on a field trip.

   Ms. Crain made an agreement with the class in which each student received a point each time he was in his seat working at the time the tardy bell rang. The points could be accumulated, and when the students had 1,500 points, the class could turn in the points and go on a field trip.

   a. How many times did Ms. Webster reinforce her students?
   b. What behavior did Ms. Webster reinforce?
   c. What is likely to be the result of the action taken by Ms. Webster?
   d. How many times did Ms. Crain reinforce her students?
   e. What behavior did Ms. Crain reinforce?
   f. What is likely to be the result of the action taken by Ms. Crain?

5. Describe how teachers can use "feedback" through record keeping to help desired behaviors become self-reinforcing.

6. Describe how you might develop a positive means for evaluating your students.

7. Ms. Williams noted that Charles is continually doing things such as sliding out of his seat onto the floor, making loud noises, and playing tricks on his classmates. What is the first question that the teacher should ask regarding the behavior? How can Ms. Williams use the answer to the above question to help her attain her positive objectives?

8. Mr. Janicky, the music teacher, is bemoaning the fact that his students only want to listen to contemporary music. How might he utilize the above information to help him solve his problem?

9. We want the behaviors contained in our affective objective to become self-reinforcing. Describe how a behavior becomes self-reinforcing. How can we utilize student record keeping and the resulting feedback to help behavior become self-reinforcing?

Attaining the Necessary Distribution of Reinforcement

The attainment of our positive motivational objectives requires that we increase the distribution of reinforcement as well as the frequency of reinforcement. It is generally true that in the traditional classroom there is not only not enough reinforcement, but the reinforcement that is there is not adequately distributed. A visit to a typical classroom usually reveals the primary reinforcement is teacher feedback indicating student responses are correct. A further observation of the situation usually also reveals a few of the students receive nearly all of the positive feedback, and many students receive almost no positive reinforcement.

Individual Differences and the Distribution of Reinforcement

The difficulty in attaining an adequate distribution of reinforcement to all students arises because of the great degree of individual differences that exist in our classroom. The cognitive and psychomotor abilities of the students in any class tend to be spread over an age span of many years. This is true regardless of the grouping system used in the school. From the point of view of a teacher involved in the design of learning experiences, there is no such thing as the first, second, third, . . . twelfth grade level. Grade level performances are just the average performance level of the students in a particular grade. The actual performance of the students varies several years on each side of the average. We are often surprised to find that about half of the students in the eighth grade cannot read at the eighth-grade level. Similarly, we are surprised to find that about 50 percent of the average class are not able to do the work typically specified for that grade. On the other hand, the upper 50 percent of the class not only contains students capable of doing the work, but contains students who have been capable of doing the work for years. It has been pointed out that when a random group of first graders enters school, their test scores on general ability (disregarding the upper and lower 2 percent) are already spread over a four-year mental age span. These individual differences, however, do not decrease with age, but instead tend to increase. The mental age span of this same group of children will have increased to eight years by the time they reach the sixth grade. Some students will be operating at the level of the average second-grade student while others will be able to perform tasks normally performed by sophomores in high school. These students are all likely to be found in the same sixth-grade classroom. Attempts have been made to reduce the individual differences found in the typical classroom by grouping students according to their abilities in specific subject matter areas. These attempts have only been minimally successful, and the ability levels in the classes still extend over several years (Goodlad & Anderson, 1959). The trend in schools, however, is away from ability grouping and toward more heterogeneous classes which have greater differences in ability. The current "mainstreaming" of special education students into typical classrooms is a case in point. The result of "mainstreaming" will be to insure the classroom teachers will have wider degrees of individual differences with which to cope. These differences will occur in all three domains--affective, cognitive, and psychomotor. Our task becomes to find ways of insuring an adequate distribution of reinforcement to all students regardless of their ability levels.

The attainment of an adequate distribution of reinforcement requires that we individualize our instruction. The individualization of instruction is a complex process, and practical classroom considerations often make complete individualization difficult. However, we have a responsibility to move as close as possible to the individualization of instruction. A complete discussion of the process of individualization is beyond the scope of this text. Suffice it to say, however, that homogeneous grouping of students according to abilities in specific subject matter areas, diagnostic tests, curriculum materials constructed at different levels of difficulty, individual projects, etc., all provide us with ways of moving toward the individualization of instruction. The difficulties involved in completely individualizing instruction do not release us from the responsibility of individualizing to the greatest degree possible. Failure to individualize our instruction inevitably leads to an inadequate distribution of reinforcement, and the subsequent motivational problems that insure that a large number of students will never achieve their potential.

Steps in Using Task Cards

Increasing the distribution of reinforcement to all students through the individualization of instruction is made easier if we will develop task cards (Homme, 1972). These task cards can then be used as the basis for developing contingency contracts with our students. This process involves the five steps discussed below.

> **Step 1.** **Begin the development** of task cards by **describing** the complex behaviors that are appropriate for the **the different levels** found in **the class.**

The development of task cards begins with the specification of the complex behaviors that the students are to be able to perform at the completion of the event. The behaviors are complex because they are a composite of a number of simpler behaviors. Some examples of complex behaviors from different subject matter areas are shown below.

1. The students will be able to solve the three kinds of percentage problems.

2. The students will be able to write paragraphs utlizing topic sentences.

3. The students will be able to balance oxidation reduction equations.

4. The students will be able to administer first aid to heart attack victims.

5. The students will be able to balance a checkbook.

6. The students will be able to trace a bill through the congress until it becomes a law.

Step 2. Break the complex behaviors down into the specific behaviors which are necessary prerequisites for attaining the complex behavior. Use these behaviors to construct specific objectives which are appropriate for the student.

The complex behaviors that we have placed on our task cards cannot be attained directly. Instead, they must be attained in a series of steps. We need to analyze these complex behaviors, and reduce them to a sequence of more specific behaviors which will accumulate to lead to the attainment of the complex behaviors.

The sequencing of the specific behaviors from simple to complex enables us to develop a corresponding list of specific objectives which can be placed on task cards. We can then arrange the task cards in a simple to complex order, and distribute them to the students for whom the objectives are appropriate.

Determining the appropriate task card for an individual requires that we know where each student is in relationship to the attainment of the complex goal. We need to know which specific behaviors the individual can perform, and then select a task card which involves learning an appropriate new behavior. The educational objective on the task card may be deemed appropriate if the psychological distance from where the students are to where they are to go is such that the gap can be bridged with a minimum of frustration. The selection of the appropriate task card will help us avoid one of our most common errors in attempting to change behavior--that of making the initial step the students must take before they are reinforced too large. The result of this error is that we never get a chance to reinforce the behavior. Most of the objectives we are attempting to attain require the shaping of behavior through the reinforcement of successive approximations. If the initial objective we establish for the student is appropriate, we will be able to reinforce the student, and it will be possible to begin the shaping process.

Below are a number of examples of appropriate and inappropriate objectives in each of the three domains.

Cognitive Domain

Current status of student	The student can add columns of single-digit numbers.
Inappropriate initial objective	The student will be able to solve addition problems requiring the addition of three, three-digit numbers.
Appropriate objective	The student will be able to solve addition problems requiring the addition of two, two-digit numbers.

Psychomotor Domain

Current status of student	The student can do 1 "pull up".
Inappropriate initial objective	The student will be able to do 10 "pull ups".
Appropriate objective	The student will be able to do 2 "pull ups".

Affective Domain

Current status of student	The student is unable to stay in his seat and study during assigned study time.
Inappropriate initial objective	The student will spend the available study time in his seat studying.
Appropriate objective	The student will spend 2 minutes of available study time studying.

If the educational objectives on the task cards that we give our students are appropriate, we will have solved a major problem in achieving an adequate distribution of reinforcement. All of the students will be able to accomplish their objective, and we will be able to reinforce them. In addition, we will have established the conditions that will allow us to avoid the signal learning experiences that tend to turn learning and learning-related activities into conditioned aversive stimuli. A natural result of this will be the subsequent reduction of student escape and withdrawal behaviors.

We need to find goals and objectives that are attainable for each student if we are to be able to adequately distribute reinforcement to each student. We cannot excuse ourselves by saying that the material is too difficult for the student. If the students cannot attain the objectives set for them, we have to reassess the objective and assign goals to them that they can attain. Major changes in student behavior come about as the direct result of many small changes. We need to recognize this, and work to keep our objective appropriate for each individual student.

Step 3. Select the learning tasks to lead to the attainment of the specific objectives. Incorporate the tasks on to the task cards, and order the cards in the manner that leads most directly to the performance of the complex task.

The third step in preparing task cards is the selection of the learning tasks to lead to the attainment of the specific objectives. The learning tasks are the basis for the day-to-day individual task assignments for each student. This does not necessarily mean that all students will necessarily be working on the same task at the same time. The difficulty of the learning task should be appropriate for the ability level of the student.

The daily task cards should preserve an orderly and continuous flow of the instructional sequence from one unit to the next. It is best if the student can successfully complete at least two task units in a class period. The completion of two or more task units each class period allows us an opportunity to reinforce each student at least twice.

Some examples of complex behaviors and the simpler behaviors that might comprise the daily task units are included below. There are many other tasks involved in each of the complex behaviors. The task units included provide only a few illustrations of the characteristics of the tasks.

1.	Complex task	Solving the three kinds of percentage problems.
	Daily task units	Change fractions to percents.
		Change decimals to percents.
2.	Complex task	Find the correct decimal place in division and multiplication problems.
		Identify new examples of simple and complex sentences.
	Daily task units	Identify the subject of sentences.
		Identify the main verb in sentences.
		Identify the direct object in sentences.
3.	Complex task	Identify political arguments based on the concept of "manifest destiny".
	Daily task units	Identify stated assumptions.
		Identify unstated assumptions.
		Evaluate arguments based on the assumptions made in the argument.

We need to collect material related to the complex tasks. These materials are used to provide the learning experiences. They can be books, magazines, audio visual materials, etc. They should be directly related to the complex behavior. The materials should be of varying levels of difficulty because they are to be used by students of varying abilities. We would be wise to get our students involved in the gathering of the materials, and then reinforcing them for providing materials.

The final step in preparing task cards for individualized instruction is to divide the materials so that they correspond to the daily task units.

In assigning materials to be used for attaining the complex behaviors, we choose materials that relate directly to the complex behaviors, divide the materials by chapter or units that correspond to the complex behaviors, and finally, assign specific pages as daily task units.

Step 4. **Find positive ways of evaluating the attainment of both the complex and specific behaviors.**

Positive ways of evaluating student performance are essential if we are to attain an adequate distribution of reinforcement to all students. Student learning requires constant evaluation in terms of feedback on the progress being made. If the students are to go on and continue to learn, the majority of the feedback they receive must be positive.

The comparative grading system used in many schools is inconsistent with the learning conditions necessary to promote the continued growth of the students. Comparative grading insures (1) that large numbers of students are constantly exposed to signal learning experiences that tend to turn teachers, subject matter, school learning, etc. into conditioned aversive stimuli; and (2) that many students receive little of the reinforcement necessary if they are to go on and continue to learn. We do not normally think of our grades as reward or punishment. We tend to think of grades as things that are earned. The grade, however, is an indication of success or failure which can function as either a positive or negative unconditioned stimulus. Consequently, the presentation of a grade is either punishment or reward depending upon how it is perceived by the student. The degree of individual differences found in every classroom insures that the grades received by many students in a comparative grading system are nearly always punitive. The result of the punitive grading is a loss of motivation and decreased learning.

The school system typically determines the evaluation system we use. We must work within the constraints of our own situation. There are, however, some actions that we can take to limit the deterimental effects of grading. One of these is to grade the student based on improvement. Grades are still used, but the individual is compared with himself rather than with other class members, who may be years ahead or behind in terms of ability in that particular subject matter area. The approach is not a panacea, but it does avoid some of the harmful effects of comparative grading.

The establishment of specific behavioral objectives puts us in a good position to positively evaluate student performance. For example, if we establish the following specific behavioral objective for Jim:

Jim will be able to do long division with two numbers in the divisor.

The best kind of positive report that we could make regarding the progress that Jim is making would be to indicate the new capability he has acquired. We could report that Jim:

> Has learned to do long division with two numbers in the divisor.

The positive report consists of indicating what the student has accomplished--not what the student has failed to do. Other examples of positive reports are:

> Sue has acquired the ability to predict the effect of various tax laws on the distribution of income.

> Edward has acquired the ability to construct paragraphs using topic sentences.

> Eileen is able to write paragraphs using symbolism.

> Fred can produce a slice serve in tennis which enters the service court 95 percent of the time.

> Bill, given a geographic map, can use established principles to predict where cities and industries are likely to be formed.

> Cheryl can now solve the different kinds of distance--time problems.

Evaluation systems that indicate the accomplishments of the students are preferable to comparative grading approaches because they communicate to the student, parents, and others, they do not involve punishment, and they allow us to maintain a positive approach to all students. When we use positive statements in student evaluations, we become dispensers of success instead of failure. The by-products of this approach are greater student learning, and an increase in our ability to reinforce desired student behaviors through personal attention.

Step 5.   Establish contingency contracts with the students.

The specification of daily task units on task cards, and the identification of materials directly related to the task units enables us to establish contingency contracts with each student. A contingency contract is an agreement or contract we make with a student in which we promise a reinforcer in return for desired student behaviors.

Contingency contracts can be made in any of the three domains. Contracts in the cognitive domain that are related to task units mentioned above might be:

1.   If you get 80 percent of the decimal equivalence problems on page 59 correct, you can play number games for ten minutes.

2.   If you can identify 75 percent of the direct objects on worksheet 18, you can go to the library for thirty minutes.

3.   If you can identify the unstated assumptions in the paragraph on worksheet 25, you can select an activity from the reinforcement menu.

The contracts listed above are concerned primarily with whether or not the student can perform the contracted behavior. Each of the above required a specific level of performance. These characteristics make the contracts cognitive rather than affective contracts.

Contingency contracts can also be concerned with psychomotor behavior. These contracts will also be concerned with acquiring the ability to perform a new behavior. Examples of psychomotor contracts might be:

1.   If you get to the point where you can jog three miles, you can skip calisthenics for two weeks.

2.   If you get to the point where you can do a front flip off the diving board, you can go swimming at 2 o'clock Friday afternoon for three weeks.

3.   If you can improve the wrist snap on your serve in tennis, you can play number two singles in the next tennis match.

The above contracts are psychomotor contracts because they emphasize the development of a new skill or ability.

Summary

The attainment of our important affective goals require that we establish positive--not negative or permissive classrooms. Positive classrooms are classrooms in which the students perform their learning tasks because of the intrinsic or extrinsic reinforcement they receive. Positive classrooms differ from negative classroom in which students perform learning tasks in order to avoid the aversive

132

consequences of not performing them. They also differ from permissive classrooms in which the ability to reinforce ultimately comes to reside with the peer-group.

Our problems in implementing affective instruction center around finding ways in which we can 1) provide the necessary frequency, variety and distribution of reinforcement, and 2) control peer-group reinforcement. More specifically, our problems are concerned with the practicality of reinforcing each student for each successive approximation of a goal, distributing reinforcement to all students, finding the necessary reinforcers in the schools and controlling peer-group reinforcement of undesired behaviors.

The establishment of classroom conditions so that our students are reinforced more frequently by a variety of reinforcers requires that we be flexible and creative.

The reinforcers are present in nearly every school system. They typically do not involve much in terms of financial expenditures; but instead, require that we break away from typical classroom procedures in which teacher feedback and grades are about the only reinforcement.

We need to increase our ability to reinforce desired student behaviors through the use of personal attention. Our smiles, complements and feedback are--and will probably continue to be, a primary source of reinforcement in the classroom. Our ability to reinforce through the use of personal attention is not constant. It is possible for us to establish conditions that increase or decrease our ability to reinforce through personal attention. If we establish negative classrooms in which the students are performing in order to avoid the aversive consequences of not performing, negative signal learning experiences are bound to follow. These signal learning experiences are likely to cause us to become conditioned aversive stimuli that cause anxiety for our students. When this occurs, our ability to reinforce our students through personal attention is diminished. Conversely, if we establish positive classrooms in which the students perform because of the intrinsic or extrinsic reinforcement they receive, positive signal learning experiences are likely to cause us to become positive conditioned stimuli. When this occurs, our ability to reinforce through the use of personal attention is enhanced.

Our ability to reinforce our students through personal attention will increase if we can learn to:

> be positive.
> associate ourselves with positive signal learning experiences.
> talk to students about their interests.
> send positive reports home.

Increasing the variety of reinforcement in the classroom, is made easier by the development of menus which contain a large number of reinforcers which are readily available for strengthening desired student behaviors. Menu items can be attained in a number of different ways. They can be attained by analyzing what we are currently doing to determine the reinforcers we are presently giving away. They can be attained by searching the surrounding community for the reinforcing activities inherent in it. Menu items can also be attained by a careful observation of student behavior. Student behaviors that are occurring with a high degree of frequency can be used to strengthen weaker behavior. Behaviors that students perform during their free time can often be used as menu items. In addition, undesired student behaviors also provide a cue to possible reinforcers. The same reinforcers that are strenthening the undesired behaviors can be used to strengthen the desired behaviors.

We also need to be creative in increasing the frequency of reinforcement in the classroom. We need to remember that the frequency of reinforcement is more important than the size of the reinforcer in changing behavior. Large changes in behavior occur more often as the result of frequent reinforcement with small reinforcer rather than from the infrequent reinforcement with large reinforcers. There are three main ways in which we can increase the frequency of reinforcement in our classroom. First, we can involve the students in keeping their own records. The frequent feedback they receive as they move toward the attainment of their goals is reinforcing. Second, we can develop reinforcement systems in which many small reinforcers accumulate to make possible the attainment of a large reinforcer. The third way that we can increase the frequency of reinforcement in the classroom is by harnessing peer reinforcement. If we can establish the conditions in our classroom so that every time a student attains an individual goal the entire class wins; we will have created the conditions that will lead to the peer-group reinforcement of desired student behaviors. When this occurs, the frequency of reinforcement in the classroom increases geometrically.

Good affective instruction requires that we find ways of distributing reinforcement to all students. In the average classroom the limited reinforcement that is there, typically goes to a few of the talented student. This situation needs to be corrected if we are to attain our affective goals.

The difficulty we have in attaining an adequate distribution of reinforcement occurs because of the great degree of individual differences found in our classrooms. The degree of individual differences in the classroom creates a situation in which nearly any goal that we establish for the entire class is inappropriate. It is inappropriate because it is too difficult for some students, and has already been attained by others. Under these circumstances, we have difficulty achieving an appropriate distribution of reinforcement to all students.

The achievement of an adequate distribution of reinforcement requires that we individualize our instruction by establishing appropriate objectives for each student, design learning experiences to help each student attain their goal, devise a positive evaluation system, and reinforce each student on an appropriate schedule for progress toward the goal. This is most easily done through the development of task cards. These cards can then be used as the basis for establishing contingency contracts with our students. The contracts are agreements that we make with our students in which we offer a specific reinforcer for the performance of a specific behavior.

Read the questions below, and attempt to answer them in a manner that explains our problems in acquiring an adequate distribution of reinforcement.

1. An observer came into Mr. Cahn's class and recorded the frequency with which the students correctly answered questions. The observer recorded the data by making a drawing of the seats in the room and recording a tally each time the student in a seat responded correctly to a question. The observations were made on several different days. However, they all closely resembled the drawing below.

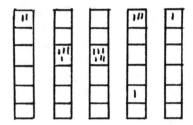

    a. What does the drawing reveal about the distribution of reinforcement?

    b. What assumptions are being made regarding the reinforcement?

2. The greatest deterrent to attaining an adequate distribution of reinforcement to all students in the traditionally run classroom is:

_____

Describe why this is so. _____

_____

_____

_____

3. When is a cognitive or psychomotor objective appropriate for a student?

_____

4. How does the use of task cards, help us utilize the process of successive approximation?

5. Describe the problem we face in the typical classroom in attempting to attain an adequate distribution of reinforcement to all students.

6. What is contained on task cards, and how does the use of task cards facilitate the individualization of instruction?

7. What are contingency contracts, and how do they work with task cards to insure a more adequate distribution of reinforcement?

8. Determine a complex behavior that you might be attempting to teach to your students. Then construct two task cards involving more specific behaviors that are necessary prerequisites for performing the complex behavior.

9. Write a contingency contract regarding the specific behaviors on the task card above.

10. What is a positive evaluation system, and how does it differ from the approach to evaluation that is currently being used in most schools?

References

Goodlad, J. I., & Anderson, R. (1959). Toward realistic standards and sound mental health. In J. I. Goodlad (Ed.), The nongraded elementary school. New York: Harcourt, Brace and World.

Fowler, S. A., Baer, D. M., & Stolz, S. B. (Eds.) (1984). Analysis. New York: Pergamon.

Hannum, J. W., Thoresen, C. E., & Hubbard, D. R. (1974). A behavioral study of self-esteem with elementary teachers. In M. J. Mahoney & C. E. Thoresen (Eds.), Self-control: Power to the person. Monterey, CA: Brooks/Cole.

Homme, L. et al. (1972). How to use contingency contracting in the classroom. Champaign, IL: Research Press.

Skinner, B. F. (1953). Science and human behavior. New York: The Macmillan Co.

Skinner, B. F. (1973, April). The free and happy student. Educational Digest.

Stamps, L. W. (1983). The effects of intervention techniques on children's fear of failures behavior. Journal of Genetic Psychology, 123, 87-97.

CHAPTER 6

HARNESSING PEER REINFORCEMENT

Behavioral Objectives for Chapter 6

When you have completed the chapter, you should be able to:

1. identify the kinds of affective goals that most require the harnessing of peer reinforcement.

2. recognize situations that are likely to result in the harnessing of peer group reinforcement.

3. recognize the conditions under which students will and will not reinforce each other for attaining educational objectives.

4. recognize what happens if peer group goals are allowed to drift.

5. recognize the effect that harnessing peer reinforcement is likely to have on students who have not been able to satisfy their need for peer approval.

6. recognize the roles played by competition and cooperation in school learning and the harnessing of peer reinforcement.

7. identify the steps necessary to harness the peer group's reinforcing power.

8. recognize the conditions under which the peer group will reinforce the behavior of a student.

9. given student responses, be able to identify the cause of the responses and the actions the teacher should take.

10. recognize what is likely to occur if a student does not help the class attain a major goal with which the class identifies.

Discovering the Problem

As a group or in small groups read and analyze the case study of Jim in Appendix C. List the positive and negative affective objectives that you would establish for Jim. After you have listed the objectives, note the primary source of reinforcement for the undesired behaivors. Does the teacher have control of this reinforcement? Why or why not? How can you change student behavior when you do not control the reinforcement? A very high percentage of the classroom problems that trouble us most are the result of peer

reinforcement of undesired behavors.   How can this be
overcome?

The Importance of Harnessing Peer Reinforcement

If our affective instruction is to be successful we need to harness peer reinforcement. Many of our most important affective goals cannot be adequately attained without the help of the peer group. The peer group can either promote or inhibit the attainment of nearly any goal that we establish, and many of our most important goals cannot be attained without its aid. The peer group is essential to the attainment of important affective goals concerned with "self-worth," "an appreciation of the dignity and worth of others," "self-confidence," as well as many cognitive and psychomotor goals.

Our task in harnessing the reinforcement potential of the peer group is to create classroom conditions in which the peer group reinforces individual class members for the attainment of educationally desirable goals (Smith & Mayer, 1978; Hamblin, Hathaway, & Wodarski, J., 1974; Van Houten & Van Houten, 1977; Frankosky & Sulzer-Azaroff, 1978).

The successful harnessing of peer-group reinforcement has the effect of greatly increasing both the frequency and distribution of reinforcement within the classroom. We need to stop thinking of ourselves as the only source of reinforcement in the classroom, and begin thinking about how we can harness peer-group reinforcement to help us attain our educational goals. As long as we are the sole source of reinforcement for the attainment of educational objectives, the amount of reinforcement possible in the classroom is limited. However, if we can find a way of getting the peer-group members to reinforce each other for attaining academically desirable goals, the frequency of the reinforcement of desired behaviors will go up geometrically, and we will be teaching in the best of all possible worlds.

The conditions necessary for harnessing the reinforcing potential of the peer group are known. The guiding principle that we must remember is that:

> The peer group, like any other group, will reinforce
> individual members to the extent that they make a positive
> contribution to peer-group goals.

Harnessing the reinforcement potential of the peer group requires that we develop reinforcement systems in which an individual not only receives reinforcement from us for the attainment of an educational goal, but also receives peer reinforcement because of making a positive contribution to the attainment of an established peer-group goal. In other words, the reward system needs to be established so that each individual can make a contribution to the attainment of a larger peer-group reward. An example of this would be a situation in which a student receives points for increasing the amount of time he spends studying during class, and at the same time, contributes points toward the attainment of the group goal of a game period on Friday.

Rules for Harnessing Peer Reinforcement

There are seven rules that we can follow that will help us establish group reinforcement systems.

Rule 1. Establish the following as an objective--The students will increase the frequency with which they encourage each other to attain their educational objectives.

By establishing this objective, and determining how frequently the students are encouraging each other prior to implementing a procedure for harnessing peer-group reinforcement, we can gather data to help evaluate the extent to which the procedure is increasing peer-group encouragement.

Rule 2. Create major reinforcing activities with which the peer group "IDENTIFIES."

The establishment of a group reinforcement system requires that the teacher find goals with which the peer group can "identify" (i.e., the majority of the class is interested in attaining the goal). An important question we often ask when confronted with the task of creating a group reinforcement system is: Can teachers really create goals with which the peer group will "identify?" The answer to the question appears to be "Yes." Athletic teams work diligently toward the goal of winning. The experience of classroom teachers has indicated that when students are required to earn the right to take part in activities such as field trips, class parties, plays, free periods, game periods, outdoor classes, picnics, etc., the activities become "identifiable goals" for the group, and the group reinforces those individuals who make a contribution to the attainment of the goals. We can use activities like these as a basis for establishing peer-group reinforcement systems.

The word "identify" in the rule is very important. If the peer group does not identify with the goals that are established, they will not reinforce individual members for making contributions toward the attainment of the goal.

The situation below illustrates what happens when we attempt to use a goal with which the peer group does not identify as a basis for harnessing peer reinforcement.

> Edward is not very well accepted by the peer group. Mrs. Connin decides to try to increase his acceptance by the peer group. Because Edward is very interested in rock music, she places Edward with a group of other students, and requires them to make a report on rock music. The other students were not interested in the report. The result was that Edward did a lot of work, and made a good report, but was not reinforced by the group. Their reaction was to "Let Edward do it."

We often expect that in a situation like the one described above the student will gain more peer-group reinforcement. However, assigning a student to a group project in which he can make a positive contribution does not insure that the group will reinforce him. They will only reinforce the student if they "identify" with the goal.

We can find educationally related goals with which the students will identify. Many of these goals are currently part of the school program. Field trips, plays, movies, games, dances, sports outings are presently taking place in most schools. These are things the students enjoy that are currently being given away. We can use these events as major reinforcers in reinforcement systems. Group contingency contracts can then be made with the class. For example, a science teacher might determine that the class would like to have more classes outside examining plants. The conditions can then be established under which they could have class outside. The teacher might determine that they could have class outside as soon as they had acquired 400 points. Points would be accumulated each time an individual student accomplished one of the individual goals (i.e., Bill hands in a neater, more complete assignment). If the peer group identifies with the goal of having class outside, they will reinforce Bill as he contributes points toward the goal by handing in neater more complete assignments.

Rule 3. Require the students to earn the right to participate in the reinforcing activities--stop giving away potential major reinforcers.

The development of peer-group reinforcement systems requires that we let students earn the right to take part in the major reinforcing activities by attaining their individual goals. We, like parents, have fallen into the trap of giving away our major reinforcers without making them contingent on the attainment of educational goals. As a result, we are often left without activities to use in building our peer-group reinforcement systems.

The giving away of potential reinforcing activities without making them contingent on the performance of desired student behaviors has had other serious consequences besides just depriving us of potential major reinforcers. First, it deprives the peer group of potential goals to work toward. The second consequence is that it deprives individual class members of an opportunity to contribute to peer group goals.

The giving away of potential reinforcing activities without making them contingent on the performance of desired student behaviors deprives the peer group of goals to work toward. Students, like the rest of us, have a greater appreciation for things that are earned than for those things received as gifts. We are finding increasingly that our gifts are either spurned or abused. School activities are either not attended or attended by students who seem more intent on destroying than enjoying them. The activities have become viewed by the students more as rights than as privileges. Arranging classroom conditions so that students are allowed to earn the right to participate in the activities creates a situation which tends to unify the class while at the same time providing us with the means for constructing peer group reinforcement systems.

142

In addition to the above, giving away activities that are potential reinforcers for the peer group deprives many individual students of a way of making a contribution to peer group goals. Many students are continually looking for ways to contribute to peer group goals, and will readily perform the behaviors that are necessary to make a contribution. All that is required are identifiable peer group goals, and someone to show them ways of advancing the goals of the group.

Failure to create goals with which the peer group can identify allows the peer group goals to drift. When this occurs, the goals of the group tend to become centered almost exclusively on sex roles and dating. The result is the peer group comes to reinforce those individuals who contribute most to the sex roles and dating activities of the group. The unfortunate aspect of this situation is that all students are not able to contribute to the sex and dating activities of the group. Students, who are immature, shy, lacking self-confidence, or physically unattractive are not able to make positive contributions to these peer group goals. It is also true that even if a student is able to make a contribution to the sex-related goals of the peer group, the activities that the peer group reinforces are not necessarily consistent with the long-term growth of the student. The sex-related activities of the peer group are important and can never be replaced, but they should not be allowed to become the only goals of the peer group.

Many psychologists view the acquiring of peer-group acceptance as a developmental task. By this they mean that it is a task that needs to be achieved or it will affect the further growth of the child in many different areas. A prime example of a student who is failing in the attainment of this developmental task is the "class clown." The clowning behavior represents his attempt to satisfy his need for peer approval. However, the clowning does not adequately satisfy the student's need for peer approval. Evidence of this is provided by the continued performance of the clowning behavior. If the behavior were adequately satisfying the need, the behavior would only be performed occasionally when the need arose. The class clown does not know how to adequately satisfy his need for peer approval and so tends to perform the same inappropriate clowning behaviors over and over again. All of the intellectual and perceptual energies of the student appear to be directed toward finding ways to satisfy the need for peer approval. Under these conditions, student growth is greatly reduced and the achievement of the developmental task is thwarted. The social isolates in the class provide another example of students who also do not know how to contribute to peer-group goals. These students are retreating further and further into themselves. If we can show these students how to make a positive contribution to peer-group goals, it would help them achieve an important developmental task, and they would then be able to continue on with their growth in other areas.

The harnessing of peer group reinforcement requires that we (1) be creative in coming up with new major reinforcers, and (2) that we stop giving away our major reinforcers and instead make the attainment of the major reinforcers contingent on each individual's attainment of his or her particular goals.

> **Rule 4.** Create conditions so that each student can contribute to the attainment of the class goal. Create "I win – you win" not "I win, you lose" situations.

Classroom conditions must be established in such a way that each student can contribute to the class goals if peer group reinforcement is to reach those students who need it most. This requires the establishment of (1) affective, cognitive, and psychomotor objectives that are appropriate for each student; and (2) the promotion of a cooperative atmosphere in which if one student wins, everyone wins, and the avoiding of "I win, you lose" situations.

The educational objectives that are established for the individual student must be appropriate if the student is to be able to make a positive contribution to the goals of the peer group. As mentioned previously, affective, cognitive, and psychomotor objectives may be deemed appropriate for the student if the psychological distance from where the student is, to where he is to go, is neither too great nor too small. If the distance is too great, the student cannot accomplish the objective, and cannot make a contribution to the goals of the class. If the distance is too small, the student is not challenged, and growth is impaired.

The harnessing of peer-group reinforcement requires that we establish a cooperative classroom in which if "one student wins, everybody wins," and avoids establishing classrooms in which an "I win, you lose" situation exists. Students are unlikely to reinforce other students with whom they are in direct competition. They will, however, tend to reinforce individuals who they view as being on their side, and who are making a contribution to their goals. There are many situations in which competition improves performance. These situations, however, all have common elements that are not present in the typical classroom. The situations in which competition improves performance typically involve individuals who are evenly matched, and who have had a large amount of previous success in the area of competition. The range of abilities present in the average classroom extends over many years. This creates a condition where large numbers of students have no chance of competing with their more talented classmates. The growth of the students is best served by establishing classroom conditions in which each student competes with himself in an attempt to improve over his past performance. If competition is used as a means of motivating students, the competition should occur between classes rather than within classes and should be done in such a way that students of all ability levels can make a direct contribution to the team goal of winning, thus establishing the conditions so each student can receive peer reinforcement.

Rule 5. **Prominently display the point accumulations that** indicate the progress the class is making toward the attainment of their goal.

The progress that the class is making toward the attainment of their goal should be prominently displayed. The usual procedure is to develop a point thermometer similar to the ones used in cities to indicate the progress that is being made toward the established goals of the various charity drives. The posting of the progress chart provides the class with continuous feedback regarding their progress. This feedback is usually very reinforcing for the class. The teacher can also gain some idea of the value the students place on the attainment of the goal by observing the behavior of the students around the chart. If the goal is highly valued by the students, the students will tend to congregate around the progress chart before and after class, and will continually ask questions about the progress being made.

The chart or thermometer that is used should contain a series of major class goals. The goals should be arranged in such a way that as soon as one major goal is attained, the students can begin working toward the attainment of the next goal. This allows us to keep the classroom running on a positive basis. The first major class goal should be one that can be attained in about a week. If the first goal takes too long to attain, students begin to lose interest. The attainment of the first goal can then be followed by goals that take progressively longer periods of time to attain. After the students have become familiar with the system, and are aware that the payoff will come, they will be willing to work for longer periods of time between major reinforcers.

The peer-group reinforcement of individual class members requires that the class be aware whenever an individual makes a contribution to the attainment of the class goal. If the class is not aware of the contribution, it cannot reinforce the student for the attainment of the particular educational objective. Teachers have utilized different approaches to let the class know when an individual has made a contribution. One approach used has been to let the students announce the points they were contributing at the beginning of each class. Another approach involved pinning paper tokens with the names of the student and the number of points contributed to the thermometer. Still another consisted of assigning each student a color and allowing the students to color in the number of points they have contributed on the thermometer or graph. If we are creative we can find a number of ways of letting the students know when a student has made a contribution. The important point is that the class must be made aware of the contributions if they are to reinforce the individual student.

Rule 6. Establish the class contracts in such a way that there is no question the group will attain the major goal.

The agreements made with the class should be made in such a way that the major goal will be attained. The only question that should be left unanswered is how long the attainment of the goal will take. The more rapidly the individual students attain their educational objectives, the more rapidly the group will attain their major goal.

The agreement with the class should be established in such a way that the class can work around inhibitors. We should resist the tendency to establish agreements such as:

> If everyone hands in all their assignments this week, we can have an activity day on Friday.

This type of an agreement usually does not last through the first day. Some student does not hand in an assignment, and immediately voids the agreement. A better agreement would be:

> As soon as the class has accumulated 500 points as a result of handing in their assignments, we will have an activity day.

This agreement makes it impossible for a few students to keep the group from attaining the reinforcing activity. Some students may be able to delay the attainment of the goal, but they will not be able to stop it.

All students should be allowed to participate in the group reinforcing activity even if they have not made a contribution. This situation bothers many of us. We feel that if the students do not contribute, they should not participate. However, the harnessing of peer reinforcement is a powerful process, and there is a danger that if we do not closely monitor it, it will have the effect of isolating some students from the rest of the class. Players on athletic teams, who do not make a contribution, are likely to be at first criticized and then ignored. The result is that they soon leave. The same kind of result can occur to students who do not contribute to the attainment of the reinforcing activities of the class. These results are too serious to be allowed to occur. For this reason, we must watch closely for students who are not contributing, and try to find ways of getting them to contribute. This is usually not too difficult once the student knows how to contribute, and stops receiving attention for not contributing. In any case, the students should be allowed to participate in the reinforcing activity, and then be brought along slowly and encouraged to contribute to the future group goals.

Rule 7. Reinforce students for reinforcing each other.

We should look for ways of reinforcing the students for reinforcing each other. This is a little difficult to do without appearing insincere. However, if we are a little creative, we can usually find ways of strengthening the reinforcing behaviors of our students through our reactions and comments.

Case Studies: Harnessing Peer Approval

Below are four case studies in which classroom teachers have utilized "Identifiable Goals" as a basis for harnessing peer reinforcement. The first two case studies involve attempts to study the effects of a common goal on the encouraging and discouraging comments of the class. The third case study is concerned with the use of a common goal and individual reinforcement to increase the frequency with which the students ask "better questions." In the fourth case study, peer group reinforcement was harnessed in an attempt to attain objectives related to classroom mangement. The follow-up phase was not done in these case studies because of short treatment time.

Case Study 1: An Indirect Approach to Increasing Peer Reinforcement

Objectives

The students will increase the frequency with which they encourage others to attain academically desirable goals.

The students will decrease the frequency with which they are critical or try to discourage the academic achievements of others.

146

<u>Subjects</u>: Eighth grade physical education class (24 girls and 34 boys)

<u>Evaluation</u>: The behaviors were recorded by teachers involved in a team teaching situation. The class was taught by two teachers and a student teacher. This situation left the teachers free to observe and record the data. The behaviors were observed and recorded for a two week period and comprised a total of six class meetings.

<u>Procedure</u>: The unit of study was trampoline and tumbling. The unit was appropriate for the project because it allowed for individual success and achievement in an area that was new for most students. In addition, tumbling activities such as pyramid building require a group effort. The class was divided into equally combined squads of boys and girls for the purpose of forming pyramids.

The students were issued cards which listed the skill to be accomplished from easiest to hardest. As the students were tested over a skill, their proficiency was recorded and points were awarded. Individual and squad totals were posted in the gymnasium so that progress could be observed.

The project was conducted for 10 weeks (2 weeks for base rate, 8 weeks for treatment). Points were awarded as follows:

Individual Points	Behaviors
5	dress, on time, cooperation with teacher and squad members
5	each skill completed
5	awarded by teacher for sincere extreme effort toward skill or goal at any time
10	to any individual who improves his score by 50 points in one week

Squad Points	
10	routine by individual
10	best squad on pyramid
5	second best on pyramid
5	any squad that uses all members
10	any squad that improves lowest individual's score by 50 points in one week

The squad and individuals showing greatest improvement in their scores during the week were allowed to select the activity on Friday.

The point totals were computed on Friday. The total point goal was 1,000. Both squad and individual points were combined in figuring the total. Combining the points encouraged group effort and peer reinforcement. The major reinforcer was a free afternoon at the recreation center which included activities of swimming, basketball, handball, weight lifting, pinball games, juke box, etc. The smaller reinforcers were the points, which were also used for grading, peer encouragement, teacher encouragement and as a basis for selecting activities.

147

Teacher Comments: I will definitely use this system again. Peer reinforcement by using a group goal with which the students identify is a great way of motivating students. This is the main advantage of this program. The motivation comes from within and from peer reinforcement rather than from the teacher.

Writer's Comments: The students were not told to either encourage or discourage each other. The behavior change that took place came because of the reinforcement system designed by the teacher.

There was no treatment designed to reduce discouraging comments. Therefore, the reduction in discouraging comments must be the result of the treatment designed to increase encouraging remarks.

The teacher did not have enough time to run a follow-up. If the data were collected by the students, the project could go on indefinitely without undue teacher effort.

Case Study 2: A Direct Approach to Increasing Peer Reinforcement

Objective: The students will increase the frequency with which they encourage their classmates to achieve academically desirable goals.

The students will decrease the frequency with which they discourage the achievements of others.

Subjects: 28 fourth-grade students in a self-contained classroom.

Procedure

Base Rate: The students kept track of encouraging or discouraging words or actions they received from others in the classroom. Students taped a chart to the inside lid of their desks.

Treatment: The class worked toward field trips. The class was told that if they encourage each other 200 times or more a day for 15 days, they could spend an afternoon at the historical museum. After this goal was achieved (17 days), a new goal was set. The students were told that if they encouraged each other 300 times or more a day for 10 days they could go to the planetarium. The goal was achieved in 11 days.

Every individual was reinforced intermittently. Approximately every other day, the teacher went around the room stopping at each desk and asking, "How many of you were encouraged by _____ today?" Peanuts and jelly beans were passed out based on how much "encouragement" the student had provided. The four students who were "most encouraging" were given badges for their desk tops which stated, "I have a SUPER ATTITUDE."

Teacher's Comments: To prevent students from inflating the total, I never counted more than 20 positive comments from any one child per day.

I don't know how high the totals might have climbed had the project not ended. Lately, they had been reaching over 400 encouraging comments per day.

The number of discouraging comments did not drop off.

Although I suspect a number of the encouraging remarks were insincere, I am equally sure that most of them were sincere--and that some good habits were formed. Even for some who "faked it" at first, the behaviors became ingrained and real later on. And, if even 10 percent of the behaviors were real, the project was worthwhile.

Writer's Comments: Data indicate an average drop of from 322 to 266 critical remarks from base rate period to treatment. This is satistically significant. Data from other studies also indicate no reduction in critical comments. There was no treatment designed to reduce the discouraging comments, and discouraging comments really are not incompatible with encouraging comments. They can both occur in a particular time span.

Case Study 3: Class Reinforcement Project--Asking Better Questions

Objectives: The students wi l increase the frequency with which they

1. ask questions that relate new material to old.
2. ask questions that show understanding.
3. state testable hypotheses.

Subjects: Eighth-grade science class.

Base Rate: The teacher used a chart containing each behavior to be graphed, and tallied the behaviors for the entire period for 21 days.

Treatment: The teacher established a class reinforcement system in which three major reinforcers--a cookie treat in class, a trip to the city park for lunch, and a science afternoon at the state park--were used. The major reinforcers were purchased using "science dollars" which are acquired by asking the kinds of questions specified in the objectives. The teacher used a "secretary" system to keep track of questions. At the end of the class, the student names and amounts were recorded by the class treasurer. Each Friday the treasurer made sure the class chart was up to date. The chart listed each student's name and contribution. A thermometer was used to keep track of the total number of science dollars that were accumulated toward the attainment of the major reinforcers.

Teacher Comments: At first, I handed out science dollars whenever the students performed the behavior, but switched to a "secretary" system because the class was beginning to have a "carnival" atmosphere. The students became more interested in receiving dollars and figuring out what might earn dollars than in any intelligent science discussion.

The secretarial job was rotated, but the secretary tended to become the best student in the class because they could follow the discussions and figure out which objectives were being attained.

Bookkeeping and rewarding must remain with the students. At first, I found myself spending a disproportionate amount of time on the system.

The most difficult thing was to get the children to understand the type of questions I was reinforcing. At first, the questions were so artificial and irrelevant. Now that most of them do understand, we are beginning to make headway with intelligent discussions. Some students are still having trouble with this.

Writer's Comments: The teacher comment that the students were becoming more interested in "figuring out what kinds of questions might earn more dollars than in any intelligent science discussion" illustrated an important point. If the questions incorporated into the objectives are those that are directly related to understanding and thinking about science, then these questions should relate directly to intelligent discussions of science. It is hard to think of a more worthwhile goal than that of having the students ask better questions. The teacher should reinforce students for trying to figure out what kinds of questions are being reinforced.

Case Study 4: Classroom Management Objectives

Objective: The students will increase the frequency with which they hand in carefully done papers.

Base Rate: Every carefully done paper will contribute one dollar to the class treasury. The requirements for a carefully done paper were that it:

1. be written in the student's best hand writing.
2. contain correct capitalization and punctuation.
3. contain name, date, and subject.
4. contain four or fewer errors.

The base rate was determined during the first week by keeping track of how many papers would have been assigned dollar signs.

Treatment: The teacher decided if the papers were carefully done, and placed a "$" sign on it if it added to the class treasury. The students checked their folders daily to see how many dollars had been attained. On Friday, the teacher went through the folders with each student, and recorded the total number of dollars on an enlarged bank book.

The major reinforcers that the class could purchase with their dollars were:

Major group goals:

$100—lunch with teacher
$200—chew gum in class
$200—call teacher by first name for one day
$200—listen to radio during class
$300—have class outside
$350—extra gym time
$400—one night homework-free
$500—class party
$500—field trip

Teacher Comments: The number of "$" earned is increasing each week. They are currently working for a class party. I try to make sure each child does contribute to the total each week. The students are back by the bank book, and counting and recounting their dollars many times a day to see how far they have left to go. The project has been a success so far. The students are excited about it. More items will be added if interest begins to subside.

Writer's Comments: Precisely defining what constitutes a carefully done paper added much to the study. The number of students congregating about the bank book to check the progress toward the attainment of their goal provides an excellent means of measuring the degree to which the students "identify" with the goal.

Summary

The attainment of many of our most important affective goals requires the harnessing of peer-group reinforcement. Affective goals concerned with developing positive self-concepts, an appreciation of the dignity and worth of others, self-confidence, etc., require the concerted effort of both the teacher and of the peer group. If goals such as these are to be attained in an efficient manner, we cannot be working at cross purposes with the peer group. Instead, the attainment of these goals requires that we identify the behaviors related to the attainment of the broader goals, and then find ways to insure that we both reinforce the desired behaviors.

The harnessing of peer-group reinforcement is an important step in the attainment of our positive goals because it allows us to greatly increase the frequency and distribution of reinforcement. As long as we are the primary source of reinforcement for the desired behavior that occurs in the classroom, the amount of reinforcement that can occur is limited. However, if we can harness peer-group reinforcement by getting the peer group to reinforce behaviors consistent with our affective goals, both the frequency and distribution of reinforcement are unlimited.

The procedure for harnessing peer group reinforcement for the strengthening of desired behaviors requires that we establish goals with which the peer group identifies. Once this is done, we can create the conditions so that each student can contribute toward the group goal by attaining a personal objective. This creates a situation where if the student is successful, the whole group wins. Under these conditions, it behooves the peer group to encourage individual students. Harnessing peer reinforcement requires that we create an "I win--you win" situation in our classrooms, instead of the "I win--you lose," condition that currently exists in most classrooms.

Practice Exercise 6-1

Get together in groups, and attempt to do the following:

1. Briefly describe in general terms the characteristics of an ideal class.

2. Incorporate the general characteristics contained in your description into affective goals that you would like to attain.

3. Break your affective goals down into behaviors that are consistent with them, and write specific affective objectives that incorporate the behaviors.

4. List the major group reinforcers that you have or are likely to have available to you. They should be reinforcers with which you think your classes would identify. In attempting to create the list of major group reinforcers, think of potential reinforcers that:

   a. were used when you were in school.
   b. are currently being given away.
   c. are available in the surrounding community.
   d. are educational and related to your particular teaching area.
   e. other teachers are currently using.

5. Use the affective goals, objectives, and reinforcers stated above to develop a group reinforcement system. In constructing the system explain the agreements you would make with the students, how you would distribute the smaller reinforcers and how the smaller reinforcers would accumulate to make possible the attainment of the major reinforcer.

6. How could you tell if the class identified with the group goals stated above?

7. How would the system suggested above allow you to establish and maintain a positive approach throughout the year?

8. Why is the system created above an "I win--you win" rather than an "I win--lose", situation?

9. How is the class to know when a student makes a positive contribution to the attainment of the major group goal? Why is it important that they know?

10. In the system above how long do you think it will take the class to attain the first major reinforcer? Why is this important?

11. Is the system created above constructed in such a way that no one student can keep the group from attaining its goal? Why is this important?

12. What are you going to do if a student does not contribute to the attainment of the major group reinforcers? Is this individual to be allowed to take part in the reinforcing activity? What do you think will happen to a student who does not contribute to the attainment of the peer group goals? How serious is this?

References

Frankosky, R. J., & Sulzer-Azaroff, B. (1978). Individual and group consequences and collateral social behaviors. Behavior Therapy, 9, 313-327.

Hamblin, R. L., Hathaway, C., & Wodarski, J. (1974). Group contingencies, peer tutoring, and accelerating achievement. In R. Ulrich, T. Stanchnik, & J. Marby (Eds.), Control of human behavior modification in education (Vol. 3) (pp. 333-340). Glenview, IL: Scott-Foresman.

Smith, E. V., & Mayer, G. R. (1978, September). The secret pal game: Students praising students. The Guidance Clinic, pp. 3-6.

Van Houten, R., & Van Houten, J. (1977). The performance feedback system in a special education classroom: An analysis of public posting, and peer comments. Behavior Therapy, 8, 366-367.

APPENDICES

155

APPENDIX A

EDUCATIONAL GOALS

These are not in any order of importance.

LEARN HOW TO BE A GOOD CITIZEN*

A. Develop an awareness of civic rights and responsibilities.

B. Develop attitudes for productive citizenship in a democracy.*

C. Develop an attitude of respect for personal and public property.*

D. Develop an understanding of the obligations and responsibilities of citizenship.

LEARN HOW TO RESPECT AND GET ALONG WITH PEOPLE WHO THINK, DRESS, AND ACT DIFFERENTLY*

A. Develop an appreciation for an understanding of other people and other cultures.*

B. Develop an understanding of political, economic, and social patterns of the rest of the world.

C. Develop awareness of the interdependence of races, creeds, nations, and cultures.

D. Develop an awareness of the processes of group relationships.

LEARN ABOUT AND TRY TO UNDERSTAND THE CHANGES THAT TAKE PLACE IN THE WORLD

A. Develop ability to adjust the changing demands of society.

B. Develop an awareness and the ability to adjust to a changing world and its problems.

C. Develop understanding of the past, identify with the present,and the ability to meet the future.

DEVELOP SKILLS IN READING, WRITING, SPEAKING, AND LISTENING

A. Develop ability to communicate ideas and feelings effectively.

B. Develop skills in oral and written English.

UNDERSTAND THE PRACTICE DEMOCRATIC IDEAS AND IDEALS

A. Develop loyalty to American democratic ideals.*

B. Develop patriotism and loyalty to ideas to democracy.*

c. Spears, H. (1973). Kappans ponder the goals of education. Phi Delta Kappan, September

C. Develop knowledge and appreciation of the rights and privileges in our democracy.*

D. Develop an understanding of our American heritage.

LEARN HOW TO EXAMINE AND USE INFORMATION

A. Develop ability to examine constructively and creatively.

B. Develop ability to use scientific methods.

C. Develop reasoning abilities.

D. Develop skills to think and proceed logically.

UNDERSTAND AND PRACTICE THE SKILLS OF FAMILY LIVING*

A. Develop understanding and appreciation of the principles of living in the family group.*

B. Develop attitudes leading to acceptance of responsibilities as family members.*

C. Develop an awareness of future family responsibilities and achievement of skills in preparing to accept them.

LEARN TO RESPECT AND GET ALONG WITH PEOPLE WITH WHOM WE WORK AND LIVE*

A. Develop appreciation and respect for the worth and dignity of individuals.*

B. Develop respect for individual worth and understanding of minority opinions and acceptance of majority decisions.*

C. Develop a cooperative attitude toward living and working with others.*

DEVELOP SKILLS TO ENTER A SPECIFIC FIELD OF WORK

A. Develop abilities and skills needed for immediate employment.

B. Develop an awareness of opportunities and requirements related to a specific field of work.

C. Develop an appreciation of good workmanship.*

LEARN HOW TO BE A GOOD MANAGER OF MONEY, PROPERTY, AND RESOURCES

A. Develop an understanding of economic principles and responsibilities.

B. Develop ability and understanding in personal buying, selling, and investment.

C. Develop skills in management of natural and human resources and man s environment.

DEVELOP A DESIRE FOR LEARNING NOW AND IN THE FUTURE*

A. Develop intellectual curiosity and eagerness for lifelong learning.*

B. Develop a positive attitude toward learning.*

C. Develop a positive attitude toward continuing independent education.*

LEARN HOW TO USE LEISURE TIME

A. Develop ability to leisure time productively.

B. Develop a positive attitude toward participation in a range of leisure time activities--physical, intellectual, and creative.*

C. Develop appreciation and interests which will lead to wise and enjoyable use of leisure time.

PRACTICE AND UNDERSTAND THE IDEAS OF HEALTH AND SAFETY*

A. Establish an effective individual physical fitness program.

B. Develop an understanding of good physical health and well-being.

C. Establish sound personal health habits and information.

D. Develop a concern for public health and safety.*

APPRECIATE CULTURE AND BEAUTY IN THE WORLD*

A. Develop abilities for effective expression of ideas and cultural appreciation (fine arts).

B. Cultivate appreciation for beauty in various forms.*

C. Develop creative self-expressions through various media (art, music, writing, etc.).

D. Develop special talents in music, art, literature, and foreign languages.

GAIN INFORMATION NEEDED TO MAKE JOB SELECTIONS

A. Promote self-understanding and self-direction in relation to student's occupational interests.

B. Develop the ability to use information and counseling services related to the selection of a job.

C. Develop a knowledge of specific information about a particular vocation.

DEVELOP PRIDE IN WORK AND A FEELING OF SELF-WORTH*

A. Develop a feeling of student pride in his achievements and progress.*

B. Develop self-understanding and self-awareness.*

C. Develop the student's feeling of positive self-worth, security, and self-assurance.*

158

DEVELOP GOOD CHARACTER AND SELF-RESPECT

A. Develop moral responsibility and a sound ethical and moral behavior.*

B. Develop the student's capacity to discipline himself to work, study,, and play constructively.*

C. Develop a moral and ethical sense of values, goals, and processes of free society.*

D. Develop standards of personal character and ideas.*

GAIN A GENERAL EDUCATION

A. Develop a background and skills in the use of numbers, natural sciences, mathematics, and social studies.

B. Develop a fund of information and concepts.

c. Develop special interests and abilities.*

List of Reinforcers Used by Teacher

The student or students will:

1. be allowed to sit in the seat of choice the next day or during the rest of the period.
2. be allowed to operate the audio-visual materials brought to class.
3. be allowed to tell the class a joke or story during the final minutes of class.
4. be allowed to choose his or her own team in the next group assignment
5. be allowed to name the groups in the next group assignment (Superstars v. Scalawags).
6. be allowed to throw out the question which he or she feels is the least fair on the next quiz.
7. be allowed to use notes on the next quiz.
8. be chosen as a student monitor during study hall.
9. receive a pass to the library during study hall.
10. be allowed to choose that evening's homework assignment.
11. be allowed to choose the next film or filmstrips to be seen by the class (teacher supplies groups to choose from).
12. be allowed to select the next student to be called upon to recite or go to the board.
13. be allowed to sit in the teacher's chair during the rest of the period.
14. be allowed to collect the assignments from other students.
15. be allowed to get a drink at the fountain.
16. be allowed to make up the new question on an oral quiz and ask whomever he/she chooses.
17. be allowed to make up a question on the next test.
18. be allowed to be office manager for one week.
19. be allowed to take 5 minute breaks for every 40 minutes of good classroom behavior.
20. have a "good news note" sent home to parents.
21. participate in ski trip planned for Fridays.
22. be able to have math contest for classes on Fridays.
23. be allowed to be flag bearer.
24. be allowed to make morning announcements on intercom.
25. be allowed to be class helper (make dittoes).
26. be allowed to be safety guard.
27. be allowed to be hall monitor.
28. be allowed to be official for after-school basketball game.
29. be allowed to be film projector operator.
30. be allowed to make paper ribbons.
31. have grade raised one point after attaining a certain number of points.
32. be able to choose a special or favorite game during gym.
33. be able to have extra gym time.
34. be able to be a special helper in art, music, gym, or kindergarten.
35. be able to attend a major league baseball game.
36. receive dittoed certificates indicating achievement.
37. be allowed playtime in the snow (K-2).
38. be allowed to be in student-faculty game (volleyball).
39. receive free time (classroom or gym).
40. not have to take the review tests.
41. be allowed to have ice skating party.

42. be allowed to have bike hike and picnic.
43. be allowed to have P.E. tournaments.
44. be allowed to be classroom teacher for one hour.
45. be allowed to have separate gym classes for boys and girls.
46. be allowed to take a trip to fire department (K-1).
47. be allowed to have a boys against girls in kickball game.
48. be allowed to have a sock hop (fifth grade girls).
49. be called fifth-grade Superstars.
50. have pictures of students in P.E. activities to take home to parents.
51. be praised in front of class.
52. be allowed to drink water during gym.
53. be allowed to have class mascot on the desk for an entire day.
54. be able to choose a classroom job for the week rather than being assigned a job.
55. not having to take the spelling test.
56. choose a night in which there will be no homework.
57. have a coded message of encouragement taped to desk in the morning.
58. help at teachers' luncheons.
59. be allowed free time at the science table.
60. be allowed to choose the recess activity on Friday.
61. be allowed to help in the kindergarten once a week.
62. not have to follow some school rule for a day.
63. be allowed to hang coat, etc. in my closet.
64. have free choice of seating.
65. receive award of the week for courtesy, cooperating, etc.
66. be able to have lunch with teacher in the classroom.
67. be allowed a goof-off day.
68. be allowed to call teacher by first name for one class period.
69. be allowed one excused tardiness.
70. be allowed permission to snack in class for one period.
71. be allowed to listen to baseball game (or some other topical event) during class period.
72. be allowed to listen to half-an-hour of popular music in class.
73. be allowed to have a movie instead of a lecture.
74. have no homework over weekend.
75. have permission to leave class early.
76. have permission to wear a hat to class.
77. be allowed to use tape recorder to tell story into, sing, joke, or whatever.
78. receive a "day off" from doing assigned seat work.
79. be allowed to go to the library or cafeteria for one period.
80. be allowed to play a game (such as checkers) with a friend during one period.
81. be allowed to use the video recorder.
82. be allowed to take polaroid pictures and put them on the bulletin board.
83. be allowed to be a messenger.
84. be allowed to be Front captain or Back captain.
85. be allowed to erase blackboard.
86. be allowed to work on model or puzzles.
87. be allowed an extra 15 or 20 minutes at the easel to paint a picture.
88. be allowed five minutes at the typewriter.
89. be allowed to pass out materials (crayons, paper, etc.) for a week.
90. be able to sit and work with whomever he or she pleases for a whole day.
91. have a chance to use my magic markers.
92. be allowed to make work charts for assignment, attendance, and behavior.
93. be allowed to help a friend do an assignment.
94. be allowed to read or tell a story to the class.
95. be allowed to water plants.

96. be allowed to sit by teacher during lunch time.
97. be allowed to take the teacher's tray back for a week.
98. be allowed to pass out napkins during lunch for a week.
99. be allowed to help other teachers.
100. be allowed to help in grading papers for a week.
101. be allowed to organize and be in charge of discussion group (group leader).
102. be allowed to participate in a special sewing group.
103. be allowed to be in charge of keeping the room tidy for a week.
104. be allowed to go to basketball game or movie free.
105. be allowed to show the whole class a movie.
106. be room librarian or assistant in the main library.
107. be allowed an extra art class.
108. be allowed to design and put up a bulletin board.
109. be allowed extra time in the learning center.
110. be allowed to be helper in office.
111. be allowed an extra gym class.
112. be allowed to clean out teacher's desk and organize books.
113. be allowed to draw mural on chalk board.
114. be allowed to do math on chalk board.
115. be allowed to chew gum and eat candy in class.
116. be allowed to use individual rugs for work or reading on floor.
117. be allowed to play teacher, correcting things in class or giving spelling test.
118. get a personal call home from teacher about good behavior or work.
119. be allowed to use a ditto to duplicate something for entire class.
120. be allowed to listen to radio--their station--during work periods.
121. be allowed to use tape recorder to tape themselves or others and listen.
122. be allowed to have a fruit break--they bring a piece of fruit and have it at a certain time.
123. be allowed to read to the lower grades or help the teachers.
124. be allowed to sit by the window.
125. be allowed to have a party.
126. be allowed to have free discussion.
127. be allowed a game period.
128. be allowed to use the overhead projector
129. be allowed to choose filmstrip to show class.
130. be allowed to use teacher's water cooler for a day.
131. be allowed to have extra recess period.
132. be allowed to have homework pass.
133. be allowed to have free cookie question.
134. be allowed to have a seat exchange.
135. be allowed to have a game period during the day (30 minutes).
136. be allowed additional time working with Supermachine (A-V for health).
137. be allowed to clean out desk during day.
138. be allowed to help put up or take down a bulletin board.
139. be allowed a free "State your State" (riddle bulletin board for social studies).
140. be allowed to be a science lab helper.
141. be allowed a washroom pass.
142. be allowed to be lunch room helper.
143. be allowed to play instruments in music.
144. be allowed to have an extra non-scheduled art period.
145. be allowed to have a 20-minute manipulative game period.
146. be allowed to tell ghost stories.
147. be allowed to bring pet to school to show class.
148. be allowed to come into building 20 minutes early in the morning and help teacher.

149. beallowedto skip multiplication quiz one week.
150. get points towards going to nearby park to play.
151. beallowedto play the piano.
152. beallowedto use typewriter.
153. beallowed to take teacher role--i.e., listen to someone read, give spelling test, or give multiplication quiz.
154. be allowed to write on blackboard during the day.
155. be allowed to collect fines for late library books.
156. be allowed to tape record voice and listen to it.
157. be allowed to decide (from list of teacher suggestions) where to go on next field trip.
158. be allowed to decorate bulletin board in teacher's lounge.
159. be allowed to help custodian clean up lunch room.
160. be allowed to run the film projector and take the films back to the AV department.
161. be allowed to erase blackboard for a week.
162. be allowed to get the water for the plants and water them twice a week.
163. be allowed to take attendance cards to the office.
164. be allowed to staple papers together, such as tests, etc.
165. be allowed to run off tests or other papers on the copying machine in the main office.
166. be allowed to correct quizzes in class and make up the scale, record the grades, all done at the teacher's desk.
167. be allowed to make up a sample quiz in the teacher's office, while listening to radio.
168. be allowed to give dictation in French to the class.
169. be allowed to bring hard candy to class for the entire class to eat while watching a movie or reading.
170. be allowed to play French scrabble, monopoly, Mille Bornes for half a period.
171. be allowed to listen to French records while reading, or just to listen to them. The last very effective for records such as: Fiddler on the Roof, Godspell in French.
172. be allowed to pursue French comic books, magazines.
173. be allowed to choose on which day of a given week a quiz is to be given.
174. be allowed to go to the library to work or do research.
175. be allowed to make a crossword puzzle or word scramble, using all the new words in a given unit.
176. be allowed to make bulletin board. This involves several students and many happy trips around the school gathering the materials.
177. be allowed to do the preparing of food for our unit on ethnic foods; this involves working in the home economics department.
178. receive attention from the teacher (verbal praise, a smile, a pat).
179. be allowed to hold the doors.
180. be allowed an extra washroom and fountain pass.
181. be allowed to be first in line (or first to get coat on, etc.).
182. be allowed double recess.
183. be allowed fr e time to read or play a game.
184. be allowed to pass out paper and supplies.
185. be allowed to be helper to clean off tables, etc.
186. have a letter of praise sent home.
187. receive a star on a chart (points).
188. be able to see a movie or puppet show.
189. have storytime (being read a story).
190. have extra time in gym.
191. be allowed to be "teacher" and sit in teacher's desk.

192. be allowed to chew gum during class.
193. be allowed to bring games from home.
194. be allowed to bring a friend to visit class.
195. be allowed to make and throw a paper airplane five times.
196. be allowed to walk around in high heels.
197. be allowed to paint at easel.
198. be allowed to pop a balloon, paper bag, or milk carton.
199. be allowed to play with a squirt gun.
200. be allowed to be team captain.
201. be allowed to read a comic book.
202. be allowed to get swung around.
203. be allowed to push adult around in swivel chair.
204. be allowed to be student teacher.
205. be allowed to read to class.
206. be allowed 15 minutes in library.
207. be allowed to return filmstrip projector.
208. be allowed to pick a story for teacher to read to class.
209. be allowed to have a day off.
210. be allowed to be classroom supervisor.
211. be allowed to have time with teacher.
212. be allowed to blow bubbles with soapsuds.
213. be allowed to visit another class.
214. be allowed to be a pen pal.
215. be allowed to skip a test.
216. be allowed no homework on weekends.
217. be allowed a field trip.
218. be allowed time to visit at the end of class.
219. be allowed occasional classes where students do what they want.
220. be allowed to arrange the order of student reports.
221. be allowed to store extra materials in classroom.
222. be allowed to bring own book for reading assignment.
223. be allowed in-class time for theme writing.
224. be allowed to help plan next unit.
225. be allowed to take books to bookstore or messages anywhere.
226. be allowed to select slides for art and architecture units.
227. be allowed to compose test items.
228. be allowed to throw out lowest grade in series of quizzes.
229. be allowed library passes.
230. be allowed to have name on posted list of achievers.
231. be allowed bonus points on homework.
232. will not have to revise a composition.
233. have a positive letter sent home.
234. be allowed to check attendance for teacher.
235. be given a ride home from the teacher.
236. receive a personal, positive call from the teacher.
237. be allowed to read newspaper last 15 minutes of class.
238. be allowed to see a movie.
239. be allowed to read Scope magazine.

APPENDIX C: THE CASE STUDY OF JIM

Jim is an eighth-grade student in my physical science class. Jim comes from a very high-middle economic social class. He often displays an attitude that he can do whatever he wants to do and that teachers cannot make him do anything that he does not want to do. His physical appearance is that of a well-adjusted boy. Jim has a physiological condition which at times causes him to be very hyperactive during class. He tends to "fool around" in class and play games with his friends. Jim is immature in comparison to other students at his grade level. In class, I have separated Jim from his friends because his "fooling around" behavior tends to disturb the class. He consistently gets out of his assigned seat and sits with his friends. At times, I have scolded him and given him a detention, but it seems to do no good in altering his behavior. In class, he tends to be inconsiderate, impolite, boisterous, and mischievous..

Jim is a very slow achiever. In the past he has received relatively few successful experiences in school. His reading level is at the fifth grade level. His attention span seems to be very short because he tends to talk or "fool around" with his friends in class while the teacher discusses the current topic. During class he puts forth no effort and hands in no work and on tests, he barely hands in the answer sheet (and fails all tests). Since he does not participate well in class, he tends to yell joking remarks to get attention. The class usually laughs at his remarks and he is reinforced in repeating his behavior. In class, the students tend to recognize and stigmatize Jim as "dumb." His peer group perceived Jim as a "Big Clown." Therefore, he usually plays the role of the "dumb clown' to get peer group approval. At times during laboratory exercises, Jim does display some interest in experiments. Since he is very hyperactive, he tends to bother other students in other groups. Students have complained about Jim being a disturbance and a nuisance.

I have talked to Jim about his behavior in class, but it seems to have no effect in altering his behavior. I have written remarks and comments to his parents about his behavior in an attempt to get some communication with them.

Many times, I have overheard Jim say to other students in class that he "hates" science. He enjoys other classes such as physical education and shop. He does average work in other classes such as English, history, and mathematics.